THE CHRISTIAN EXPERIENCE

The Christian Experience

•

James J. Mulligan

ALBA · HOUSE   NEW · YORK

Nihil Obstat:
Daniel V. Flynn, J.C.D.
Censor Librorum
Imprimatur:
+James P. Mahoney
Vicar General, Archdiocese of New York
February 12, 1973

The *Nihil obstat* and *Imprimatur* are a declaration that a book or pamphlet is considered to be free from doctrinal or moral error. It is not implied that those who have granted the *Nihil obstat* and *Imprimatur* agree with the contents, opinions or statements expressed.

Current Printing (last digit):
9 8 7 6 5 4 3 2 1

LIBRARY OF CONGRESS
CATALOGING IN PUBLICATION DATA

Mulligan, James J
  The Christian experience.

  Includes bibliographical references.
  1. Spiritual life—Catholic authors.
  2. Sacraments—Catholic Church. I. Title.
BX2350.2.M84   248'.48'2   73-4005
ISBN 0-8189-0270-1

DESIGNED, PRINTED AND BOUND IN THE UNITED STATES
OF AMERICA BY THE FATHERS AND BROTHERS OF THE
SOCIETY OF ST. PAUL, 2187 VICTORY BOULEVARD,
STATEN ISLAND, NEW YORK 10314 AS PART OF
THEIR COMMUNICATIONS APOSTOLATE.

FOREWORD

THE LAST FEW years have seen an increasing interest in theology even on the part of those who would not usually be thought of as professional theologians. This interest has also brought with it an increased awareness of some of the difficulties of theology. Its language is frequently hard to understand, many of its ideas are quite complex and its application to the problems of everyday life is not always readily discernible. This means that the task of the theologian is not a simple one, but it also means that the average reader may find that he has to have some considerable training in a new jargon and a new way of thinking before he is able to tell what the theologian means.

In writing the present book, I have attempted to indicate how theology can be put into practice. I have tried to take a number of ideas in sacramental theology and to use these as a means of understanding the practical effect of the sacraments in the life of the Christian. This effort constitutes the bulk of the book. The last three chapters are intended to take the reader into slightly different directions. The chapter on the interior life is intended to give an example of an experiential presentation of the realities discussed in the preceding chapters. In it I have attempted to summarize and explain some of the basic concepts presented by Saint Teresa of Avila in her book *The Interior Castle*. The chapter on Mary is intended to show something of the meaning of real Christian perfection in the framework of ecclesial unity in Christ. In the last chapter I have tried to present a theological foundation for all that has preceded, and so this chapter may appear a good deal more abstract than those which precede it. It is my hope that by the time the reader reaches it he will have been able to grasp more clearly the implications of his own experience, and will be able to see that what appears to be abstract is not really such. It is rather an attempt to put experience into an orderly presentation which will give a clearer idea of the way in which God has chosen to call us to himself.

It is my hope that the book will be of use to the general reader, but I would also like it to be of some assistance to the priest as well. This usefulness will, I hope, appear in his function as spiritual director. The book may suggest some ways in which people can be introduced to a life of prayer and of real sacramental devotion.

If Christianity is to be a means of salvation for all men, it must be a means that is available to all. It must be a religion that is simple enough to be found in the experience of all men, no matter how different that experience may appear to be at times. I hope that this book will perhaps contribute to this by presenting the experience of a number of people in such a way that others can also gain from it and find that it has been a real part of their own experience as well. I must also take the opportunity to express my thanks to the many priests, religious, seminarians and lay people with whom I have been in contact the last few years. Many of the ideas in the book have come from my association with them and from their experience as well as my own.

There are also a number of people who should be thanked individually. Sister Joan Bunty, osf, typed the original manuscript and made a number of very fine suggestions. Mr. and Mrs. John Boucher read the manuscript before it was published and contributed some valuable ideas. Sister Mary Kruezberger, osf, gave me some very fine ideas which were incorporated into the chapters on religious life and the Blessed Virgin. Sister Bessie Chambers, rscj, gave me a great deal of encouragement, which finally led to the publication of the work.

CONTENTS

INTRODUCTION

THE LIFE OF the Christian is a life which by its very nature involves tension. It is the life of one who should live in this world and yet be directed to another world. The Christian cannot live totally immersed in the affairs of mundane reality to the exclusion of spiritual concerns, because to do so would be to violate his being as a Christian. At the same time, he cannot isolate himself from this world and attempt to make himself pure spirit removed from all matter, because to do so would be to violate his being as a man.

The same tension can be stated another way. The Christian exists between the poles of an incarnational and an eschatological spirituality. He is already transformed, and yet he awaits the fullness of his transformation. By his entrance into union with Christ he has become a new sinless creation, and still he never loses the possibility of sin. He is in the peculiar position of awaiting a change which has already occurred. His hope is a true hope because it is directed to a reality which already exists within him. Yet he must find within himself a certain amount of fear, because he knows that he can reject the hope in spite of its presence. An exaggerated incarnational spirituality would lead him to consider himself already so in unity with God that he would lose sight of the possibility of sin. This could lead him to the brink of self-destruction and of the destruction of others, since he would not see the possibilities of harm in his actions. An exaggerated eschatological spirituality would lead him to a notion of union with God so other-worldly that he would lose sight of what has already happened to him as a Christian. This could lead him to the brink of self-destruction and of the destruction of others since he would not see the possibilities of good in his actions. The true Christian must steer a course which enables him to avoid either extreme.

Another source of tension for the Christian (really the same tension manifesting itself in another way) is the relationship between his sanctification and his immersion in the necessary routine of his daily life. He may allow daily routine to distract him from his real goal in life. Or he may allow his goal in life to distract him from a routine which is really necessary to himself and those around him. What he must do is to sanctify the routine itself, and he can only do this insofar as he is conscious in some way of the true direction of his life. His answer is to be found in transformation and not in rejection. Furthermore, different states in life may demand the transformation of different actions, and so the appearance is created of widely differing spiritualities. His choice is made more difficult by those around him, and yet it is in them that he should be finding his sanctification.

It is to this tension that this whole book is directed. Yet even here the tension will manifest itself, because it is impossible to so delineate the practices of Christian life as to make them immediately applicable to all in a univocal way. To attempt to do this would be to deny the very tension which is at the basis of the life of the Christian, and this would be to propose a system which would be applicable to none while pretending to be applicable to all. What I shall attempt to do is to indicate guidelines by means of a general discussion of basic elements in the life of every Christian. It then becomes the responsibility of the individual to find the application of these in his own life. He will not, however, find that application in isolation. It should be found through the medium of his own personality, his own needs and the needs of those around him, his choice of a state in life and the assistance of a spiritual director.

CHAPTER ONE:

BAPTISM AND CONFIRMATION

AS CHRISTIANS we have been baptized, and many of us have baptized others. Unfortunately, we don't often take the time to consider what we have done or what has been done to us. In the letters of Saint Paul there are constant references to baptism. For him it is the foundation of the Christian life and seems to be applicable to every situation in life. Yet how often do we reflect on our own baptism? How often is it considered in the sermons that we hear or deliver? And when it is considered, what is said about it? It seems to have been my experience that most of the sermons that I have heard on baptism (and they have not been very many) have spoken of the washing away of original sin. Baptism is presented as a bath which purifies us.

Saint Paul uses similar terms in his earlier letters, although he never seems to be totally limited to that concept of the sacrament. In fact, his theology is in a constant process of development, as can be seen if one reads his epistles in the order in which they were written.

Paul constantly placed his emphasis on faith as the basis of salvation. This is certainly not to be limited to a mere intellectual acceptance of facts, even though acceptance of facts is one of its elements. It is a much fuller giving of self in response to the personal communication of God in the humanity of Jesus. The correlation of faith and revelation always implies a personal relationship, some point of personal contact in both the Eucharist and baptism. In the letter to the Romans Paul places more emphasis on baptism.

Whereas we tend to think of baptismal symbolism in terms of washing and purification, Paul here sees it more in terms of re-creation. Our union with the risen Jesus is put into terms of sacramental baptism. I have already referred to our understanding of baptism as purification. This is evident in the symbol of the pouring of the water. Paul's symbolism seems rather to be based on baptism by immersion. The person goes down completely into the water and rises again. "Through baptism we have been buried with him in death, so that just as he was raised from the dead through the Father's glory, we too may live a new life."[1]

The notion of baptism as purification and washing is, of course, present in Paul's thought. He had written to the people of Corinth: "You have been washed, you have been consecrated; you have been justified in the name of the Lord Jesus Christ and in the Spirit of our God."[2] In the whole passage Paul was concerned with the morality of the people.[3] By baptism they have been separated from the sinful environment in which they were once content to live. They must now live a new life in accord with their new being. They have been transferred into a new world as a new people. They can, of course, still reject their baptismal inheritance and revert to their former sinfulness, but they are exhorted instead to treat others and themselves with the dignity and respect due to one who has answered the divine call.

In the same letter to the Corinthians, Paul had also presented even more clearly the transition from washing to death and resurrection in the baptismal symbolism. "Our fathers were all under the cloud, and all passed through the sea, and all were baptized into Moses in the cloud and in the sea."[4] In the cloud and the sea one can readily see the Spirit and the water of baptism, and in Moses can be seen Christ. Here a new people is formed. The waters now become more than a bath. It is only a small transition in thought to see the waters as saving the Jews and then closing in on them to destroy their enemies. It is a rather clear type of Christian baptism. As the waters close in and destroy the powers of evil, the Christian does indeed die to his former life. He arises a new man in a new people. Again, this understanding of the text becomes quite apparent as we realize that Paul is telling the Corinthians to avoid the old immorality because they themselves are new men.

The Christian reception of Christ in baptism has also been referred to in the epistle to the Galatians. "In Christ Jesus you are all sons of God through your faith. For all of you who have been baptized into Christ have clothed yourselves with Christ."[5] The images of washing and death and resurrection are further explained in the image of clothing. To be clothed in Christ is to share the life of Christ. Again the result is a newness of being which is clearly far more than a mere metaphor. The real principle of this new life is Christ himself.

It becomes evident now that Paul's baptismal theology in the epistle to the Romans is not a new departure. It has been developing all along. When he now proceeds to speak of the Christian's newness of life, all that has preceded becomes more explicit. The element of purification, however, is subordinated to the fact of renewal through resurrection. Baptismal cleansing is thus seen as more than accidental. The concept of washing would in itself lead one to think of the removal of some acquired impurity, so that the baptized person would be restored to a state which had existed prior to the acquisition of the impurity. It would be as though one were returned to the state of the original innocence of the first man. The concept of death and resurrection modifies this notion. Instead of restoration it becomes re-creation. The transformation is quite substantial. Man in union with Christ is not simply innocent but redeemed. This would help to explain his remaining attraction to sin and the constant danger of relapse.

Again we should note the relationship of revelation and faith. Faith is man's whole response to his redemption, so the redemption itself, the re-creation in Christ, is a revelation. We might say that the very newness of life is both revelation and faith. It is revelation in so far as given by God, and it is faith in so far as it is received by man. This will demand further explanation later, but for the moment let us listen to Saint Paul: "If we have grown into union with him by undergoing a death like his, of course we shall do so by being raised to life like him, for we know that our old self was crucified with him to do away with our sinful body, so that we might not be enslaved to sin any longer, for when a man is dead he is free from the claims of sin. If we have died with Christ, we believe that we shall also live with him, for we know that Christ, once raised from the dead, will never die again; death has no more hold on him. For when he died, he became once for all dead to sin; the life he now lives is a life in relation to God. So you also must think of yourselves as dead to sin but alive to God, through union with Christ Jesus."[6]

This new life reveals itself in new activity. The slavery to sin has been transformed into a slavery to justification. The new man lives in a consecration which leads to life eternal. The wages of his sinful life was death, but his consecration in Christ now enables him to receive the gift of everlasting life.[7]

The Fathers of the Church saw this reality in baptism. But they also had an advantage that we do not have. When we baptize it is by pouring the water and wiping it away, and this lends itself easily to the symbol of washing. The early Church baptized by immersion and symbolism was clearer. The person went down into the water and was covered over by it. It was a sign of his death. He expressed his Trinitarian faith and then rose from the water. It was a sign that he had risen from the death of his sins and had entered a new life in union with the risen Jesus. He put on new, white clothing, because he was a new creation. His glory had already begun.

In the early Church baptism was conferred usually on the Vigil of Easter (at least in the Western Church). Converts would be given their final preparation during Lent and would receive the sacrament of their resurrection to coincide with the resurrection of Christ. During the last few weeks of preparation there would be a series of sermons given by the bishop as a final part of their catechesis. In those sermons the story of the passage through the Red Sea became important. Its importance was probably based on the fact that Paul, in his First Epistle to the Corinthians, had applied this passage to baptism.[8] He had said that the Israelites in the cloud and in the sea had accepted baptism as followers of Moses.

For the Fathers of the Church this incident in the Old Testament was a type of Christian baptism. The events of the Exodus in the Old Testament were God's most outstanding act on behalf of his people. They were taken from slavery and led into the promised land. God saved them and in saving them chose to make them his own people. He became their God and they became his people.

The subsequent Jewish history of the Old Testament is a series of alternating acceptance and rejection on the part of the people. Each time that they began to reject God they were recalled to his service by the prophets. And frequently the prophets recalled them by reminding them of what God had done for them in the Exodus. The story was retold and idealized. It was explained and interpreted. Even when the Jews were sent into exile and later liberated, the exile was not seen simply as an event in itself. It was explained as a new Exodus. Once again the people had been sent into slavery for their sins, and once again God had freed them and again accepted them as his people. The exile, however, had taught them one new lesson. It had occurred not during a period of sinfulness, but during a period of one of their many attempts at reform. It was difficult at first for them to understand how God could have punished them just as they were trying to return to him. During the exile they came to the new realization that their relationship was a matter for individual concern and not simply the responsibility of the community as a whole. They also began to realize that their land was not their final blessing. The sufferings and blessings that they underwent in this life were not God's final word.

For the Christians the Exodus remained important. It remained the foundation of God's people. Yet in the first few years of Christian history it became apparent that Christianity was going to be rejected by Judaism. The necessity arose of a new Exodus, some new foundation of a new people. It was here that the events of the Exodus and baptism as a sacrament were joined together. This joining was already occurring in Paul's letters. The Fathers took the images of the Exodus and drew them out in analogy with what had happened to the Christians. The Jews passed

through the sea, and the sea closed in on their enemies and destroyed them. They were a new people in union with Moses. The
Christians passed through the waters of baptism, and the waters
destroyed the powers of evil. They became a new people in
Christ.

For Saint Paul this newness is expressed in the difference between the material and the spiritual man.[9] The spiritual man
is so transformed, he is so renewed, he is so re-created, that he
is different. He is a new creation, a new reality. Because he is a
new reality, he is also a being who thinks in a new way. He has a
new meaning and is able to interpret that new meaning. He is a
man who thinks as God thinks and who loves as God loves. He is
now capable of seeing the world in its proper relationship to God.

This becomes the source of the tension that I mentioned
earlier. In a sense, the Christian is now a sign of contradiction.
He is an ordinary man with ordinary fears and weaknesses. He is
a man who knows that he can be mistaken, and yet he will stand
before a judge and die rather than deny Jesus, because he knows
that in this he is not mistaken. He is a man capable of sin, and
yet he preaches a world which should be sinless. He is a man who
considers visible realities as unreal, and places his hope in the
reality of things that he cannot see. He is a man who says that
he rejects wealth in order to be rich. He is a man who is most ordinary, and yet believes that God has worked a miracle in him.
He is a man who worships a God who was condemned to capital
punishment. And in all of this contradiction he is convinced that
he is right. Common sense would seem to dictate that we should
live in and for the things that we can grasp and understand, and
the Christian treats that kind of common sense as folly. In its
place he offers a folly which he claims as the common sense of
God. And, perhaps most amazingly, he is and expects to be understood by no one except those who are also Christians.

Too often we are tempted to forget that we worship as God a
Jewish teacher who died the death of a criminal. When asked
the reason for our faith we can always fall back on the fact that
this man led a life which was filled with miracles. And yet, is this

really the reason for our faith? Was it even the reason for the faith of the apostles? They saw the miracles that Jesus performed, but so did the Pharisees. The Pharisees were not converted. The miracles were not enough. Anyone who is faced with the miraculous is faced with the unexplainable. He always has the choice of saying that there must be some explanation other than God, even though at the moment he may not be able to find that explanation. The real reason for our acceptance is that there is an internal change in us which enables the miracles to become intelligible. We look at things in a new way. We see in Jesus a savior and not just a miracle-worker or a teacher. We see holiness and not magic. We see God and not just a man. And we see that our acceptance of Jesus changes us. We become truly holy and happy only in so far as we truly accept him. We become in ourselves the sign of God's presence.

The completion of the Christian's union into Jesus is contained in the anointing with oil—his confirmation. In the early Church baptism and confirmation were both conferred at the same time, and the two together formed the initiatory rite of Christianity. It was only at a later date that the reception of the two sacraments was separated by any length of time. There are many lacunae in historical knowledge of the sacrament, but this is not the time to go into historical problems. Right now we are concerned with confirmation as a practical moment in our lives as Christians. The Fathers speak in terms of the imposition of hands, the gift of the Holy Spirit, sign, chrism, anointing, fragrant oil and strengthening (confirmation). While they clearly teach that the Spirit is conferred in baptism, they also speak of conferral of the Spirit in confirmation. In the Eastern churches the sacrament was referred to as the seal of the Holy Spirit. In both East and West confirmation was considered the completion of a unity which was effected in baptism. Confirmation was spoken of in terms of nutrition or irrigation of the change which had already occurred in baptism.

In the course of time other images were added. Confirmation was seen as the strengthening of the soldier of Jesus Christ.

It was the sign of the strength of martyrs. It was seen as parallel to the courage imparted to the disciples on Pentecost. It was the prophetic anointing of the Christian who had received his priestly anointing in baptism. It was also the σφραγίς—the seal placed on slaves and soldiers which showed that they were the property of their master and were under his protection.

By the Middle Ages the notion of sacramental character had been evolved. The character was found in baptism, confirmation and holy orders. It was a real change, a new spiritual power. The sacramental character of confirmation was a power which made one an adult Christian. Every sacrament is a profession of faith. The person who is confirmed receives the power to profess his faith in words as *ex officio*.[10] Though it is clear that one who is baptized must profess the faith. In baptism the Christian gave himself to God, and in his confirmation he sealed this self-giving.

Yet for the Christian baptism and confirmation are far more than merely giving oneself to God. If all they mean is that we are presenting ourselves to God, then it would seem that God gets the bad end of the bargain. The fact is that we are presenting ourselves to God, but we are no longer making a gift of sinful humanity. We are offering him a humanity that he has transformed in the sacraments of initiation. We are offering to God a humanity which has now become united to the humanity of Jesus.

In the epistle to the Romans, Paul speaks of the sin of Adam and its effect on all men. The only reason that he does this is that he wants to speak about the fact that the redemption of Christ is universal. He begins to explain that all men need Christ's redemption because all men are sinners. We cannot here enter into lengthy discussions on the current theories of original sin, but I would simply like to mention that I think that it might be somewhat of a mistake to either quote or reject Paul's statements in supporting or rejecting such theories.

In Romans 5, despite the numerous problems of interpretation, Paul is quite clearly drawing a parallel between the effects of Adam's sin and Christ's redemptive act. Paul seems to be aware of the necessity of salvation from the results of Adam's sin on all men and from the effects of the personal sins committed by all men, Jew and gentile.[11] As one offense meant condemnation for all men, just so one righteous act means acquittal and life for all men. For just as that one man's disobedience made the mass of mankind sinners, so this one's obedience will make the mass of them upright."[12] When we limit the question to adults we are left with a very significant conclusion. All men in some way share in the guilt of Adam. Beyond this they have chosen to sin personally. The fact of the Law makes their offense all the greater, and this Law is present for both Jew and gentile. It comes through Moses and the prophets, but it also comes through God's creation. In some way also Christ's redemption affects all men, but again their cooperation is necessary. In both cases there is a solidarity of race, but there is also freedom. The parallel is that Jesus is the new Adam. We have the same solidarity of humanity with him that we have with Adam. In his redeemed humanity we are also redeemed. In addition to this it is necessary that we freely choose to accept him. Our redemption is parallel to our sinfulness, in that both are due to our humanity and our free choice.

In Jesus the divinity entered into our humanity, and in Jesus our humanity can enter into the divinity. This is what Paul is expressing in terms of the material and spiritual man. In the opening chapters of the First Epistle to the Corinthians this is presented as a very real distinction. It is not just a matter of different names for those who have accepted or rejected Christ. Instead, it is a matter of a different reality, a different being, a whole different way of life. The material man finds it impossible to understand the mystery of God. The spiritual man accepts the mystery. In fact, Paul makes a point of saying that no one can understand the secret thoughts of a man except the spirit of the man. Also no one can understand the thoughts of God except the Spirit of God. And then he has the audacity to say that he, Paul, can understand the secrets of God and so can the Corinthians. This is no mere figure of speech. In their baptism they were transformed into a new being. They have entered into the life of God himself. This is the reality that was accomplished in our baptism and our choice to accept God in Christ Jesus.

We are transformed men living in a world which has not yet completed its transformation. We are men who should be without sin, and yet we live in a world which has not yet become sinless. Unfortunately, sin does not seem to have lost its attraction for us. We are filled with the awareness of what we are as Christians, and still we commit sin. We yield to temptation and then to remorse. We try to help others to avoid sin and find that we are unsuccessful. And yet we are spiritual and not material men. At times we may feel that there is need for a miracle. Yet perhaps the real reason for our lack of success is that the miracle has happened and we find it hard to recognize. The miracle which will convert the world to God is already here at hand, and we look for it in the wrong place.

During the Second World War, C.S. Lewis wrote three novels of science fiction in which there is a great deal of theological value. The main character is a man called Ransom. He is captured and taken in a spaceship to Mars, where he finds a world which has retained its holiness and in this world he realizes what holiness is. It changes his whole life. In the second book he is transported by God to the planet Venus, which Lewis refers to as "Perelandra." On this planet life has just begun. The first man and woman have been created. Ransom meets them and finds that they live a life of happiness with only one commandment to keep. They live on islands which float in a large ocean. They are allowed to visit stationary lands, but they must never stay there overnight. Into this world comes another man from Earth. His name is Weston and he is the agent of the devil, who has come to tempt the new couple to break the commandment. He begins to tempt the Lady. Ransom finds that he is expected to argue against the tempter. At first it is easy to say that they should obey the commandment because God gave it. Weston then argues that the only reason for the commandment was to test them. God wanted them to be willing to assume the initiative and become mature. If they stayed on the land and broke a commandment which was obviously silly, then they would have proven to God that they were capable of mature judgment. Ransom discovers that no matter what argument he presents, Weston always has a better one. He always sounds more logical. He is indefatigable. Gradually Ransom is worn down to the point where he doubts that he can continue.

Finally, after a long sleep, Ransom wakes up and thinks that this can't go on:

> The enemy was using Third Degree methods. It seemed to Ransom that, but for a miracle, the Lady's resistance was bound to be worn away in the end. Why did no miracle come? Or rather, why no miracle on the right side? For the presence of the Enemy was itself a kind of miracle. Had Hell a prerogative to work wonders? Why did Heaven work none? Not for the first time he found himself questioning Divine Justice. He could not understand why [God] should remain absent when the Enemy was there in person.
>
> But while he was thinking this, as suddenly and sharply as if the solid darkness about him had spoken with articulate voice, he knew that [God] was not absent. That sense—so very welcome yet never welcomed without the overcoming of a certain resistance—that sense of the Presence which he had once or twice before experienced on Perelandra, returned to him. . . . Moreover, he became aware in some indefinable fashion that it had never been absent, that only some unconscious activity of his own had succeeded in ignoring it for the past few days.
>
> Inner silence is for our race a difficult achievement. There is a chattering part of the mind which continues, until it is corrected, to chatter on even in the holiest places. Thus, while one part of Ransom remained, as it were, prostrated in a hush of fear and love that resembled a kind of death, something else inside him, wholly unaffected by reverence, continued to pour queries and objections into his brain. "It's all very well," said this voluble critic, "a presence of *that* sort! But the enemy is really here, really saying and doing things. Where is [God's] representative?"
>
> The answer which came back to him, quick as a fencer's or a tennis player's *riposte,* out of the silence and the darkness, almost took his breath away. It seemed blasphemous. . . That miracle on the right side which he had demanded, had in fact occurred. He himself was the miracle.[13]

Our answer is the same. The miracle which will change the world has already occurred. It is us. Our faith enables us to know that the transformation of the world can be left in God's hands. But we are his hands!

1. Rom 6,4.
2. I Cor 6,11.
3. For a good treatment of the Pauline thought on baptism, I would suggest the pertinent article in A. George, S.M. (ed.) *Baptism in the New Testament*, Baltimore, 1964.
4. I Cor 10, 1-2.
5. Gal 3, 26-27.
6. Rom 6, 5-11.
7. Cf. Rom 6, 15-23.
8. I Cor 10, 1-5.
9. Cf. I Cor 1-2.
10. Cf. S.T. III, q. 72, a. 5, ad 1 et 2.
11. Cf. S. Lyonnet, S.J., *La péché originel en Rom 5, 12, et le concile de Trente*, Rome, 1961.
12. Rom 5, 18-19.
13. C.S. Lewis, *Perelandra*, Macmillan, New York, 1967.

CHAPTER TWO:

CHRISTIAN TRANSFORMATION

IF WE ARE really changed in baptism and confirmation, and if we really have become the miracle of God's redemption in the world, then what should this mean to us? What are we really? What sort of change has taken place in us? And how visible should this change be?

In a sense it is true to say that in baptism we become Christians, but in another sense it might be far more accurate to say simply that in baptism we begin to become Christians. We are certainly not Christian in everything that we do! Which of us, even after baptism, can claim to be without sin? To say that we are Christians is really to say that we are in process of becoming Christians. Our union with Christ is not yet full and complete. We are a strange combination of weakness and strength.

Still, it is in this combination of weakness and strength that God is revealing himself to the world. Again I would like to turn to Saint Paul and to offer a very brief summary of his thought in order to explain what I mean. Paul seemed to have had the same problem a number of times. He was challenged by his converts and asked to prove his credentials as an apostle. Although this happened a number of times in his career, one of the major offenses was in Corinth. In the first epistle to the Corinthians you can see that there are some in the community who are beginning to form factions. Some time after he wrote this letter he came to Corinth and was forced to leave the community. Eventually he was again reconciled with the Corinthians, and it was then that he wrote the second epistle to the Corinthians. In it especially we can see Paul's attitude to the meaning of Christianity.

What sign would we expect him to offer to prove his apostolate? We might expect him to point to miracles or to the resur-

rection of Christ. Or even to point to his own hard work in the
apostolate. He could have said that his apostolate was proven by
the fact that he gave himself to the Corinthians in the fullness
of Christian love. Actually, Paul does imply that all of these
answers are true, but none of them is the final answer. Instead, the
final answer is to be found within the Corinthians themselves.
And the answer is in weakness rather than in strength.

Paul says of himself: "I put no obstacles in anyone's path, so
that no fault may be found with my work. On the contrary, as a
servant of God I try in every way to commend myself to them,
through my great endurance in troubles, difficulties, hardships,
beatings, imprisonments, riots, labors, sleepless nights, and hun-
ger, through my purity of life, my knowledge, my patience, my
kindness, my holiness of spirit, my genuine love, the truth of my
teaching, and the power of God; with the weapons of uprightness
for the right hand and the left, in honor or dishonor, in praise or
blame; considered an imposter, when I am true, obscure, when I
am well known, at the point of death, yet here I am alive, punished, but not dead yet, pained, when I am always glad, poor,
when I make many others rich, penniless, when really I own
everything."[1] "That is why I am pleased with weaknesses, insults,
hardships, persecutions, and difficulties, when they are endured
for it is when I am weak that I am strong."[2]

In baptism the Christian enters into death and resurrection
with Christ, and that death and resurrection are a continual process. They are not accomplished in a moment but in a lifetime.
Jesus is made manifest in the world in so far as the Christian continues in his death and resurrection in union with Jesus. Paul says:
"But I have this treasure in a mere earthen jar, to show that its
amazing power belongs to God and not to me. I am hard pressed
on every side, but never cut off; perplexed but not driven to despair; routed, but not abandoned; struck down, but not destroyed;
never free from the danger of being put to death like Jesus, so that
in my body the life of Jesus may also be seen. For every day I
live I am being given up to death for Jesus' sake, so that the life

of Jesus may be visible in my mortal nature. So it is death that operates in my case, but life in yours."[3]

This idea of affliction is a theme that runs throughout the New Testament. The important point, however, is not the affliction itself, but its meaning. Affliction is not simply something that the Christian must endure. For Paul it is in the very affliction that Christianity is to be found. The trials are not due to a God who afflicts those who submit to him, but to a world which cannot find it possible to accept those who have submitted to God. It is the conflict between holiness and the refusal to accept holiness.

Paul finally insists that the Corinthians themselves are the sign of his apostolate. They are the sign of the revelation of God in the world. God's revelation becomes visible in the Christian. "You are my recommendations, written on my heart for everyone to read and understand. You show that you are a letter from Christ delivered by me, written not in ink, but in the Spirit of the living God, and not on tablets of stone, but on the human heart."[4] Paul also says: "...you demand proof that Christ really speaks to me. He is not weak in dealing with you. On the contrary, right among you he exhibits his power. Even if he was crucified through weakness, by the power of God he is alive. For we are weak as he was, but you will find that by the power of God we will be alive as he is. It is yourselves you must examine. Do you not know that Jesus Christ is within you? Unless you fail to stand the test!"[5]

As Christians we actually become the revelation of God in the world. We are the miracle of God's presence. It is in us that he is to be seen by everyone. We are his revelation, because we are the new creation. Paul told the Corinthians: "If I am not an apostle to other people, I certainly am one to you, for you yourselves in your relation to the Lord are the certificate of my apostleship."[6] "If anyone is in union with Christ he is a new being; the old state of things has passed away; there is a new state of things."[7] "And all of us reflecting the splendor of the Lord in our unveiled faces are being changed into likeness to him, from one degree of splendor to another, for this comes from the Lord who is the Spirit."[8]

As Christians we have acquired an obligation. It is the obligation of revealing God to others. This is not an obligation that is added to us as something to be fulfilled. It is not as though there is added to us some obligation extrinsic to and above the fact that we are Christians. It is an obligation that belongs to what we are in union with Jesus. If we really are Christians, then we cannot help revealing God to the world. A real Christian should be very much like the prophet Jeremiah. He found that he was so filled with the word of God that it was impossible not to preach it. He said: "Thou hast duped me, O Lord, and I let myself be duped: thou hast been too strong for me, and hast prevailed. I have become a laughing-stock all day long, everyone mocks me. As often as I speak, I must cry out, I must call, 'Violence and spoil! For the word of the Lord has become to me a reproach and derision all day long. If I say, 'I will not think of it, nor speak any more in his name,' it is in my heart like a burning fire, shut up in my bones; I am worn out with holding it in—I cannot endure it!'"²

What does this mean in our daily activity as Christians? It means, first of all, that we live as Christians because we are Christians. We bear witness to what we are by means of what we do. What I mean is that our morality follows from what we have become. It is not our morality which makes us Christians. It is not our activity which moves God to save us. We can see the impossibility of this in the very fact of the relationship between divine and human causality. It is we who depend totally on God. This is true above all in an order in which salvation is offered. God saves us simply as a freely given gift. In our reception of the gift we are changed, and as long as we do not reject that gift (by falling short of it and its demands upon us) we shall live Christian lives. Sin is a sign of our failure to receive the gift properly. Any action which is not Christian is a sign that we have begun in some way to react against the change that God has made in us. To say, however, that it is not our own actions which save us is not at all to deny the moral law that binds Christians, nor is it to be taken as an indication that morality is unimportant.

I am merely saying that it is not the law or its keeping which saves us. Salvation comes from Jesus and our personal contact with him. The moral law comes from that contact and it is the fact of our being Christian which enables us to keep the law.

This morality of the Christian, the practice of his Christianity, that action of his new being, manifests itself basically in his relationship to God and neighbor. This might be expressed as a hierarchy of values which governs the activity of the Christian. If he does begin, as a Christian, to share in some way in the knowledge and love that God has for himself, then he will begin to see himself and the world in proper perspective.

This leads to detachment, but this by no means should be taken to signify disregard. The basis of detachment is a proper scale of values. The Christian should realize that no matter how important *things* may be, they can never be as important as persons. He therefore becomes detached from things and sees them in their proper relationship to his direction to God. No matter how important a thing may be, it can never become the ultimate importance in his life.

While his detachment from things leads to an attachment to persons, this attachment is valid for him as a Christian only as it also becomes detachment in relation to God. Again I do not at all mean that there is a disregard. I mean merely that his attachment to persons can never become such that it stands between him and God, or that it replaces his attachment to God. In his relationships with others he must also see them as related to God. Together with others he must live his Christianity in such a way that all are directed to final unity in the divinity. If he allows another person to replace God, then he is destroying himself and may run the risk of destroying others. It is only by seeing others as they are in their direction to God that the Christian can properly love them as he loves himself. It is only in this context that he can properly express his true love.

He must see ultimately that he is subject to God, not because God is a taskmaster, but simply because God is the very foundation of his own existence. Any rejection of subjection to God is spiritual suicide. It is the separation of the individual from the basis of his own reality. Insofar as the Christian sees this, he will also see that he is subject to the needs of others because he and they are in the same subjection to God. To reject this subjection is not only self-destructive but again may also be harmful to others.

The Christian must practice detachment from things, detachment from persons (while never losing sight of his Christian love of them) and total subjection to God as the source of his very being. These detachments (or proper ordering of reality) form the basis of Christian virtue. They are not something to be found only in the extraordinary saint, but in the ordinary Christian (if he is truly a Christian). They are the sign that he is truly living the life which is God's gift of salvation. As a sign they do not only allow him to know that he is living correctly, but they must also be visible to others. If they are lived properly they become the manifestation of God's presence in the world, which is his presence in the Christian.

Since they are a sign of God's presence, they must be the sign not only of the life of the individual but also of the life of the whole Church. They are a sign which can be present in any state in life. In the Church they may also be presented in an organized and communitarian fashion. This is the foundation of religious life in religious communities. Here the detachments become visible in the form of vows of poverty (detachment from things), chastity (detachment from persons) and obedience (detachment from self and subjection to God). In a sense they are exaggerations, but I do not mean this in any derogatory way. They are the basic virtues of any Christian, but are practiced by the religious in the most purified and austere manner. They can thus assume their greatest clarity as signs of the life of the whole Church. The value of this practice is then not merely for individual perfection; it becomes something of value for the whole ecclesial community. It serves as a sign to all Christians and non-Christians that the weakness of the Christian is his strength, because what seems to be weakness in a world of passing values is really strength in a world which will never end.

As Christians we have received the privilege and taken upon ourselves the obligation of being the place of God's presence in the world. In all that we are or all that we do this presence should be made manifest. We have a new life and new being. As this becomes more conscious it also becomes more evident to ourselves and to others. We can never again live as isolated individuals, each in his own little world, because we have assumed the responsibility of the salvation of all men.

1. II Cor 6, 3-10.
2. II Cor 12, 10.
3. II Cor 4, 7-12.
4. II Cor 3, 2-3.
5. II Cor 13, 3-6.
6. I Cor 9, 1-2.
7. II Cor 5, 16-17.
8. II Cor 3, 18.
9. Jer 20, 7-9.

CHAPTER THREE

ORDINATION AND MARRIAGE

THE LIFE OF the Christian is a life of self-giving. In fact, self-giving is the very foundation of Christianity from man's point of view. Man submits himself to God and to his neighbor because he has received God and this reception has enabled man to know that his importance is not in himself but in God.

This element of self-giving and self-sacrifice is present in all of the sacraments. In baptism and confirmation the Christian submits himself to God so that he may be transformed. He sacrifices himself as he is so that he may receive himself back in a newness of life in union with Jesus. In the Eucharist the element of sacrifice is evident. Man offers his gifts to God and those gifts are transformed. The gift represents man and the transformation is a symbol of man's transformation. In penance the Christian offers himself to God, but this time he offers himself as a sinner seeking forgiveness. Again he must sacrifice himself and return to submission to God. In the sacrament of the anointing of the sick the Christian gives himself entirely to the will of God, and is willing to give his earthly life if God should desire to take it.

In each of these sacraments there is a sacrifice, but notice that the sacrifice in each case seems to be rather directly related to the individual relationship to God. The basic emphasis is on man's direction to God. Because of this emphasis there will, of course, be a new relationship to neighbor, but this seems to follow as a corollary of the basic and primary direction. In the other two sacraments of matrimony and holy orders there is a difference. While both of these sacraments direct the individual to God, their basic emphasis seems to be on the direction of the Christian to others. Through these others he is directed to God. Because matrimony and holy orders are so similar, I would like to treat both of them together.

In the epistle to the Ephesians Saint Paul uses marriage as an example to help explain the union of Christ and his Church. Unfortunately, this text has often been taken as a statement on the theology of marriage, whereas it is in reality a statement on the Church. Paul is speaking of the fact that Christ and his Church have become one. In order to explain this unity Paul seeks an example, and the best example that he can find is that of marriage. Perhaps the confusion in understanding the text comes from the Latin translations. In them we find the statement: *Hoc est magnum sacramentum*. This has at times been translated as: "This is a great sacrament." Its real meaning is to be found in the Greek text: τὸ μυστήριον τουτο μέγα εστίν. This is properly translated as: "This is a great mystery." The mystery is the mysterious union of Christ and his Church.

However, even though this text is not intended as an explanation of marriage, there is something about marriage that we can learn from it. Why did Paul see marriage as an appropriate example? He had been speaking of the relationship of Christians to each other, and he was making the point that there must be mutual service among the Christian people. Each must treat himself as one who is at the disposal of others as his superiors. Each must subordinate himself to the needs of the others. Paul says that this mutual service is founded in union with Christ. "Subordinate yourselves to one another out of reverence to Christ."[1] It is this which leads him to the example of marriage. He says:

> You married women must subordinate yourselves to your husbands, as you do to the Lord, for a husband is the head of his wife, just as Christ is the head of the Church, which is his body, and is saved by him. Just as the Church is in subjection to Christ, so married women must be, in everything to their husbands. You who are husbands must love your wives, just as Christ loved the Church and gave himself for her, to consecrate her, after cleansing her with the bath in water through her confession of him, in order to bring the church to himself in all her beauty, without flaw or a winkle or anything of the kind, but

to be consecrated and faultless. That is why husbands ought to love their wives—as if they were their own bodies; a man who loves his wife is really loving himself, for no one ever hates his own person, but he feeds it and takes care of it, just as Christ does with the church, for we are parts of his body. Therefore a man must leave his father and mother and attach himself to his wife, and they must become one. This is a great mystery, but I understand it of Christ and the Church.[2]

Note that in this whole text the most important element is mutual service. The wife is to obey and respect her husband, but the husband cannot demand of his wife anything which does not proceed from love and his own self-sacrifice on her behalf. Marriage, by its very nature, is directed to another. This is what makes it a symbol of the relationship between Christ and his Church.

The foundation of marriage is, then, the self-sacrificing love of both husband and wife. And this love goes far beyond the superficial love of physical attraction. They say that all brides are beautiful, but there are enough homely wives to offer evidence that this statement is not universal. The man who spends months telling his fiancee that he loves her, may see her in curlers for the first time and feel like saying: "Take me to your leader!" Yet the depth of real love goes far beyond this. There may still be in the husband a love which would make him lay down his life for his wife. How many women are married to men who are real problems? They may be gamblers, alcoholics, women-chasers, and yet the wife has a love which enables her to overcome all of this in her desire to help the man. Even beyond their mutual concern for each other, the husband and wife will subordinate themselves to the needs of their children. How many parents will sacrifice their own welfare and even their own health for the good of their children? The sacrament of matrimony sanctifies and consecrates all of this sacrifice to God. The direct result of the sacrament is a mutual giving of one to the other. Its final result, for the true Christian, is the giving of husband, wife and children to God. It is a sacrament of sacrifice and mutual holiness. It is a sacrament in which one person is sanctified, not for his own good and not through efforts directed primarily at his own sanctification, but in and through the good of another. Marriage can be the eminent sign of the Christian's love of neighbor.

In this sense the sacraments of matrimony and holy orders are quite similar. Ordination is also directed to the good of others. The fact of a man's ordination is not something that is intended to enhance only his own holiness. It is not as though he now has a benefit which is not enjoyed by those who are not ordained. What I mean is that he has no advantage over them in the leading of a Christian life other than the sacramental grace of Orders. He has instead now been placed at their disposal, because his priesthood is for them. This is the result of the sacrament. He is designated for the service of the whole community and the good of his ordination is for the benefit of others. Again a change has taken place in him, a change comparable to that in baptism and confirmation. There he became a new being, a new reality. This happens again in ordination. The new being received in baptism is further specified by confirmation and orders. He is again new with the possibility of new activity. Primary in this new activity is the power to offer sacrifice (the sacrifice of Christ on behalf of the people) and to forgive sin, and both of these powers are for the good of others. His offering of sacrifice on behalf of the Church is not a private privilege, and the offering of Mass is not "his" Mass. It is the re-presentation of the sacrifice of Christ for the good of Christians.

The offering of the Mass is the offering of a sacrifice, but this is not the whole meaning of the sacrificial aspect of the life of the priest. A man who offers the sacrifice of the Mass and does not offer himself is being hypocritical. And I do not mean that he should offer himself by including himself in the prayers of the Mass. I mean that his whole life must be a life of self-giving, and this giving of self must be in the service of others. The priest is to be at the service of all men. He must sacrifice himself in all that he does. He cannot withdraw from others and still consider himself a good priest. The priest who works in a parish and just sits in the rectory and waits for calls is not giving himself to anyone. He is merely tolerating disturbances in his ordinary routine of self-satisfaction. The priest who teaches and who gives himself to his class hours and then draws back from his students in order to retire to the privacy of his non-working hours might do well to ask himself why he was ordained.

It might be well at this point to say something about the relationship between the priesthood and religious life. The religious takes vows in order to draw himself nearer to God. His reasons are basically reasons of personal perfection in a particular state in life. Certainly if he lives his life properly as a religious he is going to have an effect on others. He will affect other members of his community and the sign value of his religious life will affect all those who come to understand what he is doing. Even for those who do not fully understand what he is doing, his life can still be a sign by the very fact of its being enigmatic. Yet the first effect is on himself. His religious vows cause him to enter into a life which has become a personal expression of a particular relationship to God. The first is, and is intended to be, his personal holiness. The ordained religious, however, is somewhat different. As a religious he seeks perfection in his relationship to God, and he must also seek to express that relationship in as clear a sign as possible. Yet as a priest his whole life is directed not to his own holiness, but to the welfare of others. His ordination is for them, just as the ordination of a diocesan priest is for others. Such ordained religious as Benedictines, Carthusians and Trappists are priests of service just as much as the parish priest. The difference lies in the type of service. I think that at times this has been one of the areas which has accounted for difficulties in understanding the meaning of priesthood. Some religious orders may have, in the past, tended to ordain men primarily as "Mass priests." It was not always clear how they carried out the other-directed mission of the priest as such. This is certainly one of the factors which has led to current questioning of the role of the priest. I do not

mean that this is the only factor, nor do I mean that the questioning is therefore invalid. What I do mean, however, is that this is one of the reasons why there has been at times a tendency to lose sight of the priesthood as service.

It might also be well to point out here that in both the diocesan priesthood and the religious priesthood there are basic dangers involved and that these dangers tend to fall into different patterns. The diocesan priest can become so involved in the activity of his work that he begins to substitute activity for prayer. This constant flurry of activity can appear, on the surface, to be quite productive and yet the priest's lack of interior growth really leaves him with very little to give to others. The religious priest, on the other hand, can be involved in parish work, or teaching, or community life, and use the community itself as an escape. He can be almost lethargic in the activities of his work and salve his conscience by withdrawing for prayer and community life. He can be personable and friendly within the community and impersonal and distant outside of it. The man who truly lives his priesthood is the man who maintains the proper balance between prayer and action.

In reality marriage and the priesthood are much alike. In both there is the reception of a sacrament, but it is received more for the benefit of others than for the benefit of oneself. In both sacraments one begets new children of God. Both priest and parent are subordinated to the needs of their children. In both sacraments the eminent virtue of Christian self-giving is central, and is specified into a particular way of giving.

I would like to close this chapter by re-emphasizing the fact that I am not distinguishing layman, religious and priest on the basis of the nearness of each to God or to holiness. I have no desire to imply that the layman should be defined in the merely negative way of one who is neither priest nor religious. By the very fact of the unity in Christ in baptism, every Christian has the privilege and obligation of the highest sanctity. It is simply a question of the way in which this sanctity is to be specified and lived by each individual. It is a question of different modes of expression of the basic Christian detachment and direction to God.

1. Eph 5, 21.
2. Eph 5, 22-32.

CHAPTER FOUR

CREATIVE CELIBACY

ONE OF THE problems in speaking of marriage and celibacy is that there is the temptation to go in two different directions. The temptation is to plunge into a discussion of marriage and then into a discussion of celibacy, and finally to see the relationship of each to the life of the Christian. In my own opinion this would simply create artificial problems. Rather, I am going to try to begin from a unified view of Christian life and only then will I consider marriage and celibacy as separable.

The human person, by the very fact that he is human, is both temporal and spatial. Time and space are not just outside influences on the individual. They are modes of his existence. It follows immediately, then, that the human person is an evolving person. His existence is existence in time and space. At no one point in that existence does he have full and complete possession of the totality of his own existence. It is an existence always in movement from past to future. Man is in full possession only of that tenuous point which divides what he has been from what he will be.

At the same time, he is truly a person with freedom and responsibility. He can make himself what he will be or what he ought to be. But in so doing he must accept himself as he is. He must, in other words, assume the personal responsibility of making the free choice of becoming what he should be in order to be a person. To put it another way, by the very fact that he is a person he must be somehow creative of himself. He has no limits but the intrinsic limits of his own humanity.

God's revelation to man is actually the transformation of man into the realm of the transcendent—into the Trinitarian life which is God. Yet the supposition of his elevation into the order of the transcendent does not deny man's responsibility for himself. It increases it. Even with expanded horizons, he still has the responsibility and freedom of his self-creativity.

The individual, in the course of his life as a person, is in constant contact with other persons, all of them also under this same obligation of the assumption of personal responsibility for themselves. In so far as he prevents their own free creativity, he makes himself less a person, because he is reducing them to the level of things and through this reduction begins to remove himself from the concept of what he also is as a person.

The assumption of personal responsibility for one's own personal evolution can, therefore, include a responsibility to others. In fact, since contact with others is an essential part of human existence, there is a necessary assumption of responsibility for others as well. It is this assumption of mutual responsibility which is the concrete manifestation of Christian charity. One assumes responsibility for his neighbor, because he does indeed love his neighbor as he loves himself.

It is at this point, perhaps, that the question of differentiation becomes most apparent. How is one both to assume responsibility for himself and to assist in the fulfillment of the self-responsibility of others? One's own situation, circumstances, personality and potentialities will open up a variety of possibilities. Among the numerous choices that have to be made, one of them is the choice of being married or unmarried. This is quite clearly a question that will have to be answered on the basis of one's own capacities as well as his relationship to God and neighbor.

The evolutionary creativity of the human being and its characteristic mutuality appear quite clearly in marriage. Each of the partners begins to assume responsibility not only for the creative evolution of himself, but for that of the other as well. The creativity of marriage also includes not merely the creative evolution of the already existing persons but even the openness to the creation of a new person and the assumption of responsibility of the evolution of that person from his conception.

This mutual concern for creativity is the central focus of Christian self-giving. One "gives himself" in order to become what he is and ought to be. His self-giving is the result of the recognition that his own finiteness is unintelligible without reference to the transcendent which is God. This element of self-giving in the sacraments has already been noted at some length in the preceding chapter.

On the background of the concept of human self-creativity and of the similarity of marriage and ordination, I will now proceed to a consideration of priestly celibacy.[1] Most of what will be said can, however, be applied to the single state even for those who are not priests.

In the last few years we have been faced with a great deal of publicity given to priests who have left the priesthood because they are discontented for one reason or another. The reason given has frequently been a discontent with the life of celibacy. It was a reason that was quite extensively publicized by many of the magazines and newspapers.

The play, *A Man for All Seasons,* revolved around Sir Thomas More's struggle with his conscience. He finds it impossible to take an oath that he cannot keep. At one point he says that taking an oath is like taking possession of yourself. It is like cupping your hands and filling them with water. If you break your word, you open your hands and lose yourself. The real point of our discussion, however, is not that it is wrong to break your word. What I want to discuss is why a man should be expected to give his word in the first place in the matter of celibacy.

Basically celibacy is an expression of Christian love. If it is entered into with the intention of maintaining this state for the rest of one's life, it becomes a permanent choice and is a lasting expression, just as love of marriage is a lasting expression. It is a giving of oneself to others, and the later rejection of celibacy may be just as much a sign of rejection of love as is divorce. It is a sign that one has turned back in on himself and has somehow begun to reject others. He has turned from selflessness to selfishness,

There are two points that I would like to consider. The first is the relationship between priesthood and celibacy. The second is the relationship between celibacy and creative love.

It seems to me that there is frequently a misunderstanding about the nature of a vocation to the priesthood. It is often looked upon simply from an internal point of view. It is treated as though God inwardly calls a man to the priesthood in some secret, internal manner, and the man then makes this vocation known to the bishop who will call him to orders when he has determined that the candidate does have this internal call. This attitude, however, makes the call to orders quite subjective. It would mean that the candidate does really have this call in some private way. It would then be entirely possible that there would be many who would have this internal call from God, but who were not called to orders by the bishop. This would certainly be detrimental to the Church and its welfare. Yet it would be totally unavoidable, unless every bishop were considered infallible in his judgment about the vocation of each candidate.

I would suggest that the correct understanding of vocation is that it is a call to serve the Church. Men are called to serve as they are needed. The candidate presents himself to the bishop for judgment, but it is very much a judgment of the candidate's qualities and capabilities. He presents himself to the seminary both for the formation and consideration. On the basis of the judgment of his capacities, he is either called or not called by the bishop, and it is this call which is the real vocation to the priesthood. It is in this that the candidate is actually called to serve the Church as a priest. I do not mean that there is no internal aspect at all. But the internal aspect is comprised of the capacities and the desire to present oneself. This internal movement however cannot be brought into external actualization without the action of the bishop. Ultimately, then, the call is external and is based on the needs of the Church as expressed in each diocese or religious community.

When we apply the notion of celibacy to each of these notions of vocation, we are left with the possibility of two very different attitudes. Celibacy may be looked upon in both a positive and a negative manner. The negative viewpoint would see celibacy as a giving up of something. It would be the rejection of marriage and family and would seem to be a form of Christian penance. From this point of view one gives up home and family and looks forward to reward in another life. Celibacy is a burden, but it is accepted willingly and from high, spiritual motives. From the positive point of view celibacy is something quite different. The conjugal act, of itself, is an intimate expression of personal conjugal love. This love is mediated through a human "materialization."[2] It is an expression of love essentially related to the function of human generation. Celibacy expresses this love in another way, and without a means essentially related to human procreation. It seems obvious that this is not a dichotomy between the material and the spiritual, nor between natural and supernatural. Certainly the celibate must "materialize" his love and use the things of this world to express his love of God and neighbor. Likewise, the married person must surpass the limits of mere "materialization" if he is to accomplish the same end. However, while the expression of love may differ, in both instances the primary element is the giving of oneself to God and to neighbor.

The primary element of celibacy, therefore, must be that of selfgiving. Because this is full and personal self-giving, the intention of a life of celibacy may be solidified by a vow or a solemn promise of some sort. This self-giving is of such a nature that it consequently excludes a conjugal relationship. Therefore, the negative notion of celibacy is incomplete. The sacrifice of wife and family is not the essence of the state of celibacy, but is merely a negative consequence. Abstinence from sexual activity is not the essence but the effect of celibacy. It is the consequence of a free and positive choice. The negative notion is thus intelligible only if seen as the natural consequence of the positive notion.

The treatment of virginity (celibacy) in the Scriptures and in the traditional teaching of the Church would lead us to conclude that celibacy is a charismatic vocation and is possible only for those who are called to it. Paul says, for example: "I should like to have everyone be just as I am myself; but each one has his own special gift from God, one of one kind and one of another. To all who are unmarried and to widows, I would say this: It is an excellent thing if they can remain single as I am. But if they cannot control themselves, let them marry."[3] One thing that certainly seems to follow from this is that celibacy should never be imposed on anyone against his will.

Celibacy is, therefore, a charismatic vocation with positive value. It is, like marriage, a true human value. Its negative consequences flow from a positive and overwhelming dedication to a goal which excludes all else.

> Celibacy, like marriage, is meaningful primarily in human terms. Both can be lived for the sake of the kingdom of God. Thus both can be undertaken as states of life that have Christian significance, too. This means that, in the first instance Christian celibacy is not the giving up of a natural value (marriage) for the sake of, and with one's eye on, a supernatural value. In the first instance celibacy is not a "supernatural value" but a possible state of life on a human level, which involves a special dedication to a particular value. It is not a matter of a choice between God and a possible marriage partner. God and the marriage partner are not competitors for our religious love; they do not set up a choice for our love, as if a true and pure love of God were possible only if one relinquishes a human partner.[4]

If we treat the vocation to the priesthood as purely internal, then we must, of course, say that it is charismatic in the same way as is celibacy. If, then, we find a person in the Western Church who is called to the priesthood but not to celibacy, we must conclude that something is wrong. Since the mistake is obviously not on the part of God who imparts the charismatic vocation, it must then be in the position of the Church. Our logical conclusion is that celibacy should not be imposed upon clerics, since to do so may be to thwart a charismatic call to the priesthood. It may put a man into a situation that he will eventually find impossible. On this basis we can say that the requirement of celibacy for all clerics is not justified and that it should be made optional. I would contend that this argument is fruitless from its inception, because its foundation is the concept of the purely internal call to the priesthood.

When we see the vocation to the priesthood in terms of the external call to service in the Church, the whole line of reasoning changes considerably. In this instance the call to celibacy still remains charismatic. Yet the requirements for the call to the priesthood must be determined by competent authority within the Church, in accord with the needs of the times. What the Church is demanding, then, is that all its candidates to the priesthood have the charismatic call to celibacy. The ultimate call to orders is external. If a man is to present himself for this call, he should first be sure that he has all the necessary qualifications demanded by those whose responsibility it is to give that call. The present discipline of the Western Church is to choose its priests only from among those who have the charismatic call to celibacy. It is not, therefore, a demand placed upon those called to the priesthood. It is, rather, a condition which should be fulfilled by those who wish to present themselves in order to be called. Its relationship to the call to orders is, then, *ante factum* rather than *post factum*. Father Schillebeeckx, for example, writes:

> As a charisma, celibacy can only be accepted in freedom, never directly or indirectly imposed, not even by the ecclesiastical hierarchy. The priestly office itself could certainly be imposed upon the faithful by Church authority on the basis of Christian obedience. But in such a case, Church authority could never impose celibacy as the condition for the reception of orders, for that would be an indirect way of making a charisma obligatory. In actuality, the Church leaves her members free in their choice of the ministry. Can the Church in this case then decree that it will ordain only those who feel themselves personally called to religious celibacy, and in that sense establish a *law* of celibacy?[25]

> Some people think that the *law* of celibacy is strictly an *obligation* to celibacy. From the foregoing, it appears that on close inspection this is an unfortunate, formally inaccurate expression, strictly speaking. The Church obliges no one to celibacy. It simply cannot do so; or if it tried, it would be overstepping its authority. This is evident in the canon providing that no one may receive higher orders unless he has previously stated (since 1931, in writing) that he *freely* embraces

religious celibacy. And on the other hand, no individual member of the Church has the *right* to an ecclesiastical office. Admission to the ministry is concretely, at least in the final instance, a matter for the Church's hierarchy to decide (cf. Acts 1:24), guided by the Spirit (Acts 20:28).[6]

Therefore, that the Church or any part of it would demand celibacy in its clerics is in no way contradictory to the true notion of vocation. Present discipline in the Western Church demands a double vocation, the one internal and charismatic in order for a man to present himself for consideration, the other external and sacramental in order for him to be ordained.

Priesthood and celibacy are not necessary correlatives. This is obvious in the fact that the Eastern Churches ordain married men. Yet even in the Eastern Churches there has been a constant tradition of the value of celibacy, although it is usually practiced in the monastic state. The connecting link between celibacy and priesthood would seem to be the sign value of celibacy-for-a-reason. It is not as though celibacy in itself expresses a value which does not exist elsewhere. Rather, it is a case of celibacy acting as a sign which points to a value applicable to all men. Father Schillebeeckx says:

> If one puts oneself at the service of this value to such an extent that one wants to remain unmarried, this voluntary celibacy becomes a *sign* expressing a sensitivity to value which exists in all mankind. Such a celibate does not thereby claim a monopoly on this fundamental value, but on the contrary becomes an effective sign and exponent of a quality which ought to flourish in everyone. To the advantage of all, he thus keeps this universal sensitivity-to-value alive and activates it.[7]

Could the Western Church change its requirement of celibacy as a condition for candidacy to orders? Certainly it could. Should it? This can be answered only by practical needs and circumstances. In any case, this question should not be of personal concern to those who have already made this choice. Those who have already committed themselves to celibacy have done so freely and have chosen to express their Christian love in this manner. Any discussion is simply a consideration for the future needs of the Church. Any change in legislation would not make a change in the value of celibacy in itself, even though it would allow for a married clergy.

One of the points that has often been brought up in the last few years is that the candidate for orders is not old enough at the time of the reception of orders to make a lasting decision of celibacy. While this may in certain cases be true because of some lack of maturity, the statement as a general condition seems to be based once again on the negative attitude to celibacy which sees it as an imposed burden and a penance. If it is seen as an expression of love, then it is no more impossible to make when a man is in his mid-twenties than it is for him to decide to marry then. In either case he has made a free choice and a choice to which he willingly binds himself for life. In both cases the motive should be that of love.

What then of the priest who is already ordained and has committed himself to a celibate life and who now wants to change that commitment? Father Karl Rahner writes:

> I do not inquire what the Church should do if a priest comes to her asking to be freed of his obligation for good reasons—or bad ones. Let us hope that the Church will feel she can safely be magnanimous in such cases. No doubt it is a great disappointment, and quite inconsistent with the sense of personal responsibility beyond all legalism (otherwise so much invoked nowadays), when a priest feels that everything is "all right" once the Church has freed him of his obligations. There is a responsibility to God from which even the Church cannot deliver a man. But as I say, I am in favour of the Church's being really magnanimous. And I shall enlarge on my views that the present vogue for getting emotional and melodramatic over the unhappiness, the distress, the torments, the frustration of many priests is craven and senseless escapism. Do not be dismayed or hoodwinked by it. Very often—I do not say always—such situations are not bare facts but the consequence, not antecedent, of a choice that must be answered for. The choice may be made tacitly and unawares, by falling away from a firm will to really operative faith, sacrifice, renunciation, prayer—a will to resist our hunger for tangible happiness.[8]

The call to Christian self-giving is the call to Christian love. It is the call to give oneself totally to God and to neighbor. It is a call to selflessness. The question that each individual must decide is how he is to answer that call. One of the choices that he must make is whether he will answer it in marriage or in celibacy. This is not a decision that can be made in the abstract. One cannot look at celibacy as an ideal in itself and on that ground alone decide that it is for him, nor can he do this with marriage. He must see the values of both marriage and celibacy, but he must see them in relationship to himself. He must decide which is better *for him*. This is not a choice that can be made without real self-knowledge.

> Hence it is clearly incorrect to pose the following dilemmas: God or mankind; nature or supernature; human or Christian; flight from the world or concern for the world; direct or mediated relation to God. These things are not opposed to each other in Christianity. So a life presenting itself as directly and exclusively dedicated to God, without human or worldly intermediary, is an unchristian illusion.[9]

> Celibacy is a choice, but it is a choice between two possible states of Christian life, not *formally* between a natural and a supernatural value. Because the value in question is as such a religious one, the choice of this kind of celibacy actually implies that one gives up a human value because one wants to realize another value. Any voluntary celibacy implies a giving-up, but celibacy "for the sake of the kingdom of God" concerns religious value in itself: that is its specifying characteristic. Directly religious celibacy thereby acquires a transcendent quality, incomprehensible from a purely secular point of view: the transcendence of the religious dimension itself. *Religious* celibacy is for this world an insoluble question mark; that is why it brings (negatively, in and through that actual giving-up) the eschatological world-transcendence or gratuity of grace into visible expression.[10]

In marriage the Christian expresses his selfless Christian love in his devotion to wife and family. He is directed to God through them and they are directed to God through him. He finds that by concentrating his love in one person or in one family he is better able to open that same love to others. Many persons who get married are, before their marriage, a bit selfish. They are often still in the process of surpassing that type of selfishness which is characteristic of childhood and adolescence. Yet many find that in marriage they discover such love in husband or wife that it changes their lives. They want to share their happiness with others. Their love gradually becomes more expansive. They are now willing to become involved in other people's problems, because they have become more selfless and are quite willing to give of themselves to others.

On the other hand, there are those who find that the best way for them to express their selfless love is in a more general way. They too must overcome an initial selfishness, and this is often overcome for the priest or religious by means of the community life of the seminary or religious community. They find that they can best express their love by not centering it on one person. This can be seen in truly holy priests, religious and laity whose lives are totally dedicated to others. They spend themselves in the service of others and in this they find their true happiness.

In both lives there are risks. The married couple run the risk of becoming so centered in each other that they become selfish and neglect others. They may even begin to treat each other as things instead of persons, each being interested only in what the other can give. This is a risk that is always present when love is centered in one person. It is a risk that can be overcome and is overcome in a truly happy marriage.

The celibate, on the other hand, runs the risk that by not centering his love in one person he may become impersonal. He can so generalize his love that it becomes little more than a kind of formality. He can become selfish and self-centered. He can begin to look to his own welfare and neglect others. This is a risk that is always present when love is not centered in one person. It is a risk that can be overcome and is overcome by the truly happy celibate.

If we insist on seeing celibacy in a purely negative fashion, we can easily become selfish. If we insist on seeing celibacy as imposed from without, we can live with it as a burden. If we see

celibacy as an expression of selfless love, then it becomes productive and no burden at all. It becomes truly Christian. It is only at
this stage that it really begins to become creative celibacy.

Celibacy is not a life for the one who is totally unattracted to
marriage. The person who would not make a good husband or
wife would probably find the same problems as a celibate. Such
problems must first be overcome before he can make an intelligent choice. Celibacy is for the person who has made a mature
decision between two possible ways of expressing his Christian
love.

1. The primary books and articles consulted in the preparation of this sec-
tion were the following:
Paul VI, *Sacerdotalis caelibatus,* June, 1967.
Joseph Blenkinsopp, *Celibacy, Ministry, Church,* Herder and Herder, 1968.
David P. O'Neill, *Priestly Celibacy and Maturity,* Sheed and Ward, 1965.
Joseph Fuchs, S.J., *De castitate et ordine sexuali,* Rome, 1959.
Edward Schillebeeckx, *Celibacy,* Sheed & Ward, 1968.
Karl Rahner, S.J., *Servants of the Lord,* Sheed & Ward, 1968.
Michael Gallagher, *Ave Maria,* Nov. 2, 1968, pp. 9-11.
Louis J. Putz, C.S.C., *Ave Maria,* Nov. 2, 1968, p. 12.
Eugene C. Kennedy, M.M., *Ave Maria,* Nov. 2, 1968, p. 12.
James Mahmer, *Ave Maria,* Dec. 7, 1968, pp. 22-24.
Thomas W. Klewin, *Pastoral Life,* Nov., 1967, pp. 605-609.
John A. O'Brien, *Pastoral Life,* Nov., 1967, pp. 611-614.
William P. O'Connell, S.J., *Pastoral Life,* May 1968, pp. 275-279.
Raymond A. Tartre, S.S.S., *Emmanuel,* June, 1966, pp. 242-246.
Bishop Alfred Ancel, *Catholic Mind,* Nov., 1967, pp. 27-37.
Robert T. Gill, O.S.A., *America,* June 10, 1967, p. 837.
John J. Evoy, S.J., *America,* July 29, 1967, p. 114.
Editorial, *America,* Dec. 24-31, 1966, pp. 821-822.
Editorial, *America,* Nov. 12, 1966, pp. 576-578.
2. Cf. Fuchs, *op. cit.*
3. I Cor 7, 7-9.
4. Schillebeeckx, *op. cit.,* p. 94.
5. Schillebeeckx, *op. cit.,* pp. 116-117.

6. Schillebeeckx, *op. cit.*, pp. 119-120.
7. Schillebeeckx, *op. cit.*, p. 95.
8. Rahner, *op. cit.*, pp. 150-151.
9. Schillebeeckx, *op. cit.*, p. 92.
10. Schillebeeckx, *op. cit.*, pp. 106-107.

CHAPTER FIVE:

RELIGIOUS LIFE

EARLIER I SPOKE of the obligations of all Christians to the ideals of poverty, chastity and obedience—at least in the sense that they must not be ruled by things, that they must recognize their own dignity and holiness and that they must submit themselves to the will of God in the salvation of the world. I would like now to take those same concepts and develop them a bit more in relation to the life of the religious.

As a preliminary, I should also note that I am speaking of religious life in the same wide sense it is spoken of in the Second Vatican Council's "Dogmatic Constitution on the Church," Chapter VI.[1] Religious life, first of all, is not being treated as a third state in addition to the lay and clerical states. Rather, it is a form of life which can be chosen by either lay persons or clerics and in which one commits himself in some permanent form to the three "evangelical counsels" of poverty, chastity and obedience. One does this in conjunction with a specific community. In the paragraphs which follow I will also speak of "vows," but I am using this word in a wide sense to refer to vow, oath, promise— various forms of public, permanent commitment.

The Second Vatican Council, in its "Decree on the Appropriate Renewal of the Religious Life," places the foundations of religious life in the baptismal consecration of the Christian.[2] The entrance into religious life involves a more specific consecration of a particular way of carrying out that baptismal call to perfection. However, to speak of the religious life as a way of perfection is not to say that only the religious can attain perfection, nor that only the religious is bound to strive for perfection. From all that has been said up to this point, it should be evident that all Christians are called to perfection in Christ. This perfection is indeed a gift, but to speak of it as a gift of God is also to say that it is an obligation. Rejection of the gift would mean rejection of God and his goodness, and this would be sinful. Striving for perfection, then, is the privilege and duty of every Christian, according to his state in life.

In the second chapter I referred to the vows of the religious as "exaggerations," and I explained that I did not intend this in a derogatory sense. It is religious life which takes the poverty, chastity and obedience demanded of all Christians and, in a certain sense, draws them out to their logical conclusions. It attempts to live these values in such a way that they become more readily visible in the life of the religious. In this way they can become a sign to the world, and this concept of sign value is quite important in an understanding of Christianity and religious life. Christianity always involves signs and symbols, and it is through signs and symbols that it makes the presence of Christ felt in the life of the individual. In this sense it might not be at all inappropriate to recognize a kind of sacramental significance in the living of religious life, even though the religious vows as such are not consecrated by a sacramental sign in the strict sense. Yet, if religious life is to have its value as sign, then those who live this life must be sure that they have not taken their vows in a negative sense.

The Christian virtue of poverty does not simply mean lack of money and property. A person can be totally without wealth and still not have the virtue of poverty. A person who has nothing and yet spends his time and efforts totally on the acquisition of things because he wants wealth is not practicing poverty. The religious, in carrying out his vow of poverty, must put things into proper perspective and live a life which makes it clear that his ultimate values are not material. All Christians must do this in their use of things. The religious does it by renouncing freely his right to the personal possession of things. This apparent negation is merely the most visible element of his positive resolve to practice the virtue. What he has comes to him from his community; he no longer has full control over what he uses.

What is really important in the religious practice of poverty is that the individual realize what he is doing. Obviously he will still have to use material things in order to live, but he must begin with the realization that he has renounced independent ownership of them in order to present a sign to the world of true Christianity. In other words, he has chosen to do something and not merely to give something up.

Along with this awareness of the value of poverty for the individual, there should also be a clear idea of community poverty. There seems to be a misconception in the concept of poverty when the individual renounces independent personal ownership and yet never wants for cars, books, radios, televisions, clothes and food. He can still very easily run the risk of becoming overly attached to things, and this will interfere with his expression of poverty, even if such things belong to the order rather than to himself. Likewise, the wealth and property that belong to the community or order should be put to the best possible use for Christianity. Nor do I think that the best possible use is investment simply in order to make more money. All of us must be careful that we do not attempt to practice poverty for ourselves, and then find ourselves involved in a kind of institutional avarice that undermines the real virtue that we are attempting to practice. This, it seems to me, can be a real problem for the person who transfers his own natural inclination to possession into a community-minded type of possession that is far from virtuous, and yet gets disguised by the altruism that seems to appear on the surface.

I would also like to make it clear that in what I have said about poverty I am not attempting to pass judgment on others. Let each judge himself. But I do want to emphasize that the judgment should be on the basis of the real spirit of poverty that is the virtue, and not merely on the basis of the presence or absence of possessions.

Chastity is also a virtue that must be practiced by every Christian, within his state of life. Chastity, as a virtue, is not the abstinence from sexual activity. It is rather the proper conduct of that activity in relationship to the meaning of Christianity. It is practiced by the married and the single both, although in different ways. It finds its foundation in the awareness of the holiness of one's own person and the person of others.

The religious practice of chastity takes the form of a vow to live in the single life. What I said of the meaning of celibacy in the priesthood applies equally to the religious. At the same time, the individual who chooses this form of life should be fully aware that he has chosen it in order to dedicate himself totally to God and neighbor. It should be a form of life that allows the individual to offer himself more completely in the service of a greater number of people. He may make this offering in a life of prayer which is rather solitary, or he may make it in an active life such as that of teaching—but in either case the fact that the individual is unmarried and without a family should make him more open to the needs of others. And when I say that he should be more open to the needs of others, I mean those both within and without the community.

What I really want to emphasize is this: The person who enters the religious life and remains, therefore, unmarried, is doing this for its positive value. The element of abstinence from sexual activity is not the major element of the virtue of chastity, nor is it the major element of the vow. It merely follows the major element, which is complete giving of oneself to God and neighbor in the form of an unmarried life. The married person gives himself to God and neighbor in and through his partner and family. The religious gives himself to God through his dedication and service to all the children of God, beginning with the members of his own community. In this sense I would say that the religious who shuts himself off from others and lives in his own world is, in some sense, failing to live out his vow of chastity.

Obedience is also a virtue of every Christian. He is first of all obedient to the needs of the children of God and especially to the needs of the Church, the Body of Christ. In the same way the obedience of the religious is not an escape from responsibility for his own actions. It is a complete assuming of responsibility in order to place himself at the disposal of the needs of the Church. It is an act of submission to his superiors, but it is not an escape.

It should be a functional obedience, with the ultimate function of working together in attainment of the goals of the community, which are, in their own way, identified with the goals of the Church in bringing all men to Christ.

There will always be the possibility that there will be some conflict between superiors and those over whom they are placed, and it is here that there is the need for the greatest possible mutual charity. There is much valuable discussion at present on the need for consideration of the individual as a person, and this is a real necessity. The superior should never forget the personal needs of those in the community. At the same time, those who live in obedience should never forget the personal needs of the superiors. It is true that obedience will be demanded quite often in areas that seem rather arbitrary. But is this not to be expected? If it were an area that were absolute and not arbitrary, guidance would hardly be necessary. And to say that something is arbitrary is to say that when it becomes a matter of community concern, then someone must be able to make decisions for the good of all concerned.

Obedience remains free because it is freely entered into and freely given. It is not blind or unreasoning. I mentioned above that obedience should be functional, and this is one of the factors that prevents blindness and unreason. By this I mean that obedience is not offered just for the sake of taking orders. This would be senseless and would be a rejection of personal rsponsibility. The superior should not give orders simply for the sake of giving orders. There should be a reason. And that reason should always involve the welfare of the individual, the community and the Church. Obedience should be the real effort to unite individual wills into the will of God, in order to accomplish the fulfillment of all things in Christ.

All proper Christian living is a way of perfection, and this is also the case with religious life, whether it be a life of contemplation or of action. The individual chooses this way of life as a means of his own personal perfection, but he must never forget that his own personal perfection is always directed to the completion of the perfection of the Body of Christ. This is where the sign value comes into play. The religious life should become a presentation of the purest elements of Christianity to the whole world. These are the same elements that are found in the life of every Christian, although in ordinary daily life in the world these elements may be obscured somewhat by the fact that the life does seem so ordinary and commonplace—even when it is a life of the greatest sanctity. The religious stands apart from the commonplace as a sign and reminder of what every Christian really is.

In what I have said so far, I am speaking of all religious—men and women, contemplative and active. I have spoken of the need for the religious as a sign and for the need to serve others, but I see no conflict between these things and the life of the contemplative. There is no way in which anyone can escape obligations to others, and this is true of the contemplative as well, who lives in community and who must be aware of the needs of the members of that community. It would also be well for the religious involved in a more active form of apostolate to keep in mind that he also has the obligations to his own community. He cannot immerse himself in his apostolate and forget the needs of the persons with whom he lives. When he begins to recognize in himself the danger that he is involved in his apostolate to the point where he is actually escaping from his own community, then he should also realize that this is an indication of some failure in growth as a religious. He should be equally aware of obligations in both directions and of the fact that both sets of obligations are part of his personal movement to fulfillment in Christ. Neither community nor apostolate can be rightly used as a form of escape.

Up to this point I have been speaking in very general terms of the ideals of religious life. I would like now to point to some more particular factors of religious life, but what I am going to say will be directed primarily to women religious. The reason for this is that, as I explained in the introduction to the book, this is a book which is based on experience (both my own and that of many others) and which is intended to appeal to experience. My own experience, in terms of spiritual direction, conferences and days of recollection, has been more with women religious than with men. What I am going to say, therefore, will appear as more directly related to them. I do not doubt, however, that these particular points are found in religious communities of men, or are, at least, paralleled in them. Once again, then, I ask the reader to make the applications for himself.

We live in a time of reform within the Church, and this reform has a considerable effect on religious life. When efforts at reform first began among religious, they often tended to focus on external factors, such as dress, customs, daily schedule, etc. If they had remained only at that level, the reforms could have ended up with very little lasting effect and could, in fact, have conceivably been rather detrimental to the real spirit of religious life. I do not mean this as criticism, since I think that reform often begins with externals since they are the most obvious realities at times. But I think that the experience of the last few years has resulted in a greater deepening of the concern for reform, and a greater realization of the realities involved.

Probably one of the first things that struck most communities was some change in the religious habit. And for many this was the first indication of the fact that externals had become quite important, frequently too important. The particular habit that was being used had become more than just a recognizable sign of identity, and many found it extremely difficult to adjust to new clothing. Yet most passed through this without much real difficulty.

A deeper reality was touched upon in communities in which there was some change in the forms and routine of prayer. One of the results of change was that the individual now found herself assuming a greater share of responsibility in her own prayer life. Some discovered, much to their dismay, that they had been faithfully taking part in community prayers without really praying. Removal of some degree of support of the community left them with a terrible feeling of emptiness and with little or no desire to pray by themselves. For some it was, in a sense, almost like starting over at the beginning, and this was also the point at which many first realized their own need for some sort of spiritual direction. The lesson to be learned from this, I think, is not a lesson of whether or not all prayer should be scheduled, but a lesson of the need to understand the importance and meaning of personal prayer. Whether prayers are rigorously scheduled or not, the religious must understand their value. Even when they are scheduled they must continue to be more than just routine. This is again an area in which spiritual direction can be of great assistance, but I will speak of that in a later chapter.

Another area which produced important results was that of changes in the style of authority and obedience. Both began, through reform of external forms, to be exercised in a manner that left considerably more room for personal choice and personal initiative. Many, at first, found it difficult to assume the responsibility for their own decisions, even in areas that were of relatively small importance.

It would seem to me that in each of these areas the element of community support that had been removed was an element that should have been removed. In its place was a new kind of community support, arising not from the rather artificial factors of schedule and vicarious decision-making, but from a deeper concern for the development of the individual within community, a concern for the assumption of personal responsibility and personal growth.

There is, of course, much more that could be said in this area of personal growth. Some of it is referred to in other chapters of this book. What I have said elsewhere of the growth of the individual in his sacramental spirituality is intended to be equally applicable to the religious. There is also a whole psychological side to these same questions, but I do not intend to enter into them in the present work. In the notes appended to this chapter I have suggested some further reading.[3]

Up to this point I have spoken primarily of religious life in terms of the vows. I think, however, that something further should be said about community. Community is more than just an occurrence. By this I mean that the religious community is not merely a group of people who have taken the same vows and just happen to live together. The community itself plays a most important part in the fulfillment of the religious life. There are mutual responsibilities of the community for its members and of the members for the community. Some of these responsibilities, of course, appear in terms of the unified effort of the members of community in the carrying out of its goals. But there are also responsibilities of equal depth in terms of the Christian life of each member.

In some ways community is much like a family. We are born into a family without any opportunity to choose who its members shall be. In the process of interaction with the members of our own families we grow to adulthood, and so each member of the family and the family unit itself has some responsibility for the growth of each individual as a Christian. In a sense, the same thing should happen in religious life. The members of the community do choose the community into which they wish to enter; but their assignment to particular houses is most often not a matter of choosing the persons with whom they wish to live. Persons of widely differing talents, inclinations, levels of development and stages of growth are drawn together into the one family. Their continued development becomes interdependent, and each has something important to contribute. The local community group becomes an intrinsic factor in the continued unity in Christ. The religious house should not become just a place to live, but should in some way become the family of each member. It is together that they will grow as religious; together that their vows will find real fulfillment; together that they will support each other in the process of Christian maturity. Those moments of crisis that every individual undergoes during his life can find some additional support in the religious family. And I would emphasize once again that this support should not be limited to the rather artificial support of rule alone; it should, instead, be the support that arises from a real concern of each member for the others. To a great extent it is this mutual support of community that makes the vows a living possibility. The vows are very hard to live in their fullness when we try to live them in isolation. They too easily become self-centered and quite sterile. Community helps to maintain life. It is this fact of community which also helps to express a sign value that could not really be expressed in the same way by an individual who binds himself to vows, but without entering into a definite community.

I would like to add just one more point to what has already been said. The life of the religious should begin with the realization that the love of God is the foundation of all life, and I refer not to our love for God, but to his love for us. It is this love which takes the initiative in all salvation and in all life leading to God.[4] It is also the realization of this love which leads religious life to become what it should be, a life of joy, peace and love. Do not misunderstand me. I do not mean that religious life will become a utopian existence. It won't. All of those who live in it are human and still in process of growing into union with Christ. But, in spite of the difficulties of human life, religious life can still begin to express that joy, peace and love that are part of the life of every Christian. And here again religious life can express it in a manner that sets it apart as a sign to all.

The ultimate goal of religious life, and hence of all renewal and reform, is imitation of Christ and union with God. It is, therefore, only true renewal of spirit which will give life to all other renewal.[5] It can occur only in that same Spirit who gives meaning to the lives of all Christians.

1. Vatican II, "Dogmatic Constitution on the Church," (*Lumen gentium*), nn. 43-47; cf. Walter M. Abbott, SJ, *The Documents of Vatican II*, Herder and Herder, 1966, pp. 73-78.
2. Cf. Vatican II, "Decree on the Appropriate Renewal of the Religious Life" (*Perfectae caritatis*), n. 5; cf. Abbott, *op. cit.*, p. 470.
3. One general approach to individual growth within community that I

would recommend highly is found in Dr. Thomas A. Harris' book, *I'm OK—You're OK,* Harper and Row, N.Y. As for books dealing more specifically with the problems of religious life, I would recommend: E. O'Doherty, *Vocation, Formation, Consecration and Vows,* Alba House, Staten Island, N.Y., and R.J. McAllister, *Conflicts in Community,* St. John's University Press, Collegeville, Minn.

4. Cf. Vatican II, *Perfectae caritatis,* n. 6; cf. Abbott, *op. cit.,* 470-471.
5. Cf. *ibid.,* n. 2,e; cf. Abbott, *op. cit.,* p. 469.

CHAPTER SIX:

THE PRIEST IN
CONTEMPORARY SOCIETY

THERE ARE THREE areas on which I intend to concentrate in this chapter. The first of these concerns current attitudes toward the priesthood; the second is the Second Vatican Council's Decree, *Presbyterorum ordinis,* on the ministry and life of priests; and the third is problems of the ministry.

A few years ago I received the report of the personnel board of one of the dioceses. In the report was a series of questions which, in my opinion, were a good reflection of some of the attitudes toward priesthood at the present time. There was, first of all, a series of questions that had been asked by a personnel consultant. These questions were then followed by another series that had been asked by the members of the board. The questions of the consultant were concerned with the sacerdotal and secular roles of the priest. The questions on the sacerdotal role asked: What are the essential attributes and qualities that are singularly characteristic of the priesthood and which, therefore, distinguish the priesthood from all other vocations? What are the generic attributes and responsibilities that are unchanging and intrinsic to the priesthood? The questions on the secular role asked: What are the social and economic conditions of the environment which are antithetical to Christian precept and practice? Exactly what is the obligation of a priest to identify with these problems and with people oppressed by social injustice and ignorance? What is his leadership role in efforts to resolve "un-Christian conditions"? The personnel board noted that the answers given to these questions differed considerably in different age groups of priests. The board then asked its own questions. They asked, first of all, whether it was important for the priests to develop a one-group type of thinking as to the sacerdotal and secular aspects of their ministry. Is one-group thinking essential for a strong framework of clergy? It is vital to have a one-group type of performance and to project a one-group image to the lay community? Or does the current situation call for open admission of differing views among priests as to their concepts of ministry? Is open divisiveness in opposition to the priestly role? Does the situation call for tolerance and sincere effort to see in a fellow-dissident's views his interpretation of how he should practice his ministry in relation to the secular world of problems?

I think that it should be noted, first of all, that an analysis of the two series of questions shows that they are not really concerned with the same thing. The second series of questions gives the impression that we must choose between a unified and a diversified point of view. It gives the impression that the one eliminates the other. It also makes one think that the unified point of view imposes itself on all without regard for their individuality and that the diversified viewpoint can exist merely because each differing point of view is tolerant of the other's existence. This, however, does not seem to have been the intent of the first series of questions. The problem there was the coexistence of the unified and the diversified. The problem of the first series of questions was that while there may be diversified ministries, there must also be a common denominator which gives meaning to the diversification. In other words, the personnel board deals with priests. In spite of every diversification of ministry, what then is that common ministry which pertains to all priests? What is the role of priest as priest—the role that he brings to bear on every diversification of ministry? And in view of that common denominator, what must then be said of diversity? How much diversity can there be without negating that which is always common to the role of the priest? Here is our basic question, and it is this question to which I would like first to address myself by examining some of the statements contained in the Council's decree on the ministry of priests.

The Council begins by considering the "Priesthood in the

Mission of the Church." Its basic emphasis is on the Eucharistic sacrifice. It is to this that the mission of the priest is directed. The Council says:

> Through the ministry of priests, the spiritual sacrifice of the faithful is made perfect in union with the sacrifice of Christ, the sole Mediator. Through the hands of priests and in the name of the whole Church, the Lord's sacrifice is offered in the Eucharist in an unbloody and sacramental manner until He Himself returns.[1]

The basic ministry of the priest is sacrificial. The Council also takes up the traditional concept of the priest as a man "set apart in a certain sense,"[2] but emphasizes that this does not mean that he is separated from others. He is set apart only in the sense that he is to be totally dedicated to his task. This task is and remains sacrificial, at least in the sense that the priest always stands before others as a sign calling them to the fullest giving of themselves to the Father.

The second chapter of the decree considers "The Ministry of Priests." In this section the Council begins by stating that the priest as co-worker with the bishop has the primary duty of pro-claiming the gospel of God to all. This means that the priest must be in contact with the needs of the people, and that he must apply the gospel to the concrete circumstances of life. He cannot merely preach in the abstract. Yet even here the Council points to the Eucharist as central. The word of the preacher is needed to give life to the reception of the sacraments, and this is most true of the bond between the Liturgy of the word and the Liturgy of the Sacrifice in the Mass. The Council says: "In this celebration, the proclamation of the death and resurrection of the Lord is in-separably joined to the responses of the people who hear, and to the very offering whereby Christ ratified the New Testament in His blood. The faithful share in this offering both by their prayers and by their recognition of the sacrament for what it is."[3]

The function of the priest is also inseparable from that of the bishop. It is in the ministry of the priest that the bishop is made present to the people of his diocese. Ministry in disobedience to the bishop is impossible. The Council says:

> By baptism men are brought into the People of God. By the sacrament
> of penance sinners are reconciled to God and the Church. By the oil of
> the sick the ailing find relief. And, especially by the celebration of
> Mass, men offer sacramentally the sacrifice of Christ. In administering
> all the sacraments, as St. Ignatius Martyr already bore witness in the
> days of the primitive Church, priests by various titles are bound to-
> gether hierarchically with the bishop. Thus in a certain way they make
> him present in every gathering of the faithful.[4]

Notice that the Council here speaks of the "administration" of the
sacraments. This is a term that can readily lend itself to a wrong
understanding. It can convey the impression of a kind of cold and
functional activity. I think, however, that if we really understand
the sacraments as actions of Christ and his Church it is not at all
wrong for the priest to think of himself as an administrator—at
least it is not wrong if the priest realizes that his administration
never means merely that he is a functionary performing assigned
tasks. He administers because he serves the needs of others. He
is a minister because he is a servant and is at the disposal of
others, and this is most true in the service that he offers sacramentally. He administers because he cares for those things which belong to the Church and are not simply his personal belongings.
This includes not simply property but even his function as a sacramental servant to the people.

There is some discussion today about the position of ex-
priests in the service of the Church. But many of the ex-priests
have never left their parishes. They have simply withdrawn from
people. They no longer give themselves. This self-giving must, of
course, take on a sacramental significance. The priest who sees
his apostolate as a vague kind of do-good sociological endeavor
and has forgotten his sacramental role has failed in his priesthood.

I do not mean that the priest's sacramental role consists simply
in dispensing sacraments as though he were a mechanism for fulfilling the requirements of matter and form. I do not mean that

the priest who hears confessions for an hour on Saturday and says Mass every day is fulfilling his priesthood. What I do mean is that the priest's primary role can be understood in sacramental terms and his other activity can be understood as having this end in view. He does not merely give absolution. Rather, he does all in his power to help others see the active mercy of God and desire it. He tries to convert them from sin to sanctity. He does this knowing that he has it within his power to serve them not simply by making them sorry for sin but also by absolving them of sin. He draws them to a realization of self-sacrifice for others, because he knows that he has the power to consecrate their gifts and so to unite them with the one sacrifice of Christ. He does not attempt to convert others to a vague kind of humanism, or to a half-hearted and vague Christianity. Rather he draws them to their sacramental entrance into the Church in baptism. He does not simply see his ministry to the sick as an apostolate to little old ladies in wheel-chairs, but he tries to understand the needs of the sick and dying and to bring them to an awareness of the cross and resurrection. And he can do this also sacramentally in the anointing of the sick. The priest who sees sociological or psychological needs of others, and thinks that he can solve their needs simply by being a sociologist or a psychologist has missed the point entirely. He has become an ex-priest. In the sacraments he has the means of bringing happiness to others. He has the means of helping them see in themselves possibilities that transcend the limits of this world. It is his constant ministry of word and example that gives meaning to his ministry of the sacraments. This kind of sacramental ministry is a full-time job. No matter what diversified aspects the priesthood may take, and I do not at all deny the multiplicity of possibilities, it is the sacramental ministry which is and remains the common denominator. And in this he can never ignore the need of his own vivid awareness of relationship to God and neighbor—an awareness that will never be there without a real life of prayer.

Up to this point I have based my remarks to a great extent on the decree of Vatican II. In that decree, the priesthood was considered basically in Eucharistic terms (a point of view which I have tried to expand into a wider sacramental one). At this point I would like to expand the concept of ministry a bit further, thus, I hope, opening up even further possibilities of diversification. I will try to do this by pointing out some of the ideas expressed in Father Raymond E. Brown's excellent book, *Priest and Bishop: Biblical Reflections.*[5]

The first half of Father Brown's book is concerned with the qualities that we tend to associate with priesthood and the way in which those qualities emerged from the Scriptural period of the Church's existence. These qualities have their origins in the priesthood of the Old Testament. If we look at the basic characteristics of this Old Testament priesthood, we find that it is at first a family priesthood and then gradually develops into a professional one. It is also hereditary and belongs to the tribe of Levi. This professionalism, however, does not remove the ideal of holiness. Even though the priest inherits his office, he is still expected to be a man who stands out as having at least a ritual holiness. We should also note that when holiness becomes merely ritual and formalistic, the prophets are quick to object and to demand holiness as an internal reality. The quality of internal holiness is most important and is never abandoned in the Old Testament. It is an ideal held out for the priest and, indeed, for the whole people.

The functions of the priest in the Old Testament also carried over into the New Testament period. Most basically we might say that the functions consisted in acting in the position of mediator between God and man. There were three areas in which this was done. The first area was in making known the will of God. This was done by means of casting lots, but it was the priest who was considered as having the ability to do so. By the time of the period of the kingdom in the Old Testament, this was a function that was taken over by the prophets as the priesthood became increasingly more formalistic (although it was no longer done by casting lots). The second function of the priest was that of teacher. This was the function that led eventually to the codes of priestly laws by which Israel and Judah were governed and are found in the books of Exodus, Leviticus, Numbers and Deuteronomy. This law, especially in Deuteronomy, was presented in the form of an exhortation to real spirituality. We read, for example: "For this charge which I am enjoining on you today is not beyond your power, nor is out of reach; it is not in the heavens, that you should say, 'O that someone would ascend to the heavens for us, and get to know it for us, and then communicate it to us, so that we may observe it!' Nor is it beyond the sea, that you should say, 'O that someone would cross the sea for us, and get to know it for us, and then communicate it to us, so that we may observe it!' No, the matter is very near you, in your mouth and in your mind, for you to observe."[6] This function of teaching was also something that was transferred from the priests, and, by the time of the New Testament period, it had been taken by the scribes. Both of the functions that were just mentioned were in the direction of God to man. The third function was from man to God. This was the function of the offering of sacrifice. By the New Testament period the first two functions had shifted over to the prophet and scribe, and so it was the function of offering sacrifice which had become most characteristic of the Israelite priesthood. The common factor in all of these functions, however, was that of mediation.

When we move from the Old Testament into the New Testament writings we find, first of all, that there are no references to Christian priests. The word for priest in Greek is ἱερεύς and is applied to both pagans and Jews, but not to Christians. Instead we find that there are two other words which are applied to Christians. These are πρεσβύτερος, meaning "elder," which is sometimes incorrectly translated as "priest," and ἐπίσκοπος, which means "overseer" and later came to refer to the office that is now held by the bishop.

By the time of the Second Century, we begin to find references to Christian priests in some of the writings, such as the

62   *The Christian Experience*

Didache. A little later we find them in Tertullian and Hippolytus. In other words, the use of the term came only gradually. Father Brown writes:

> For the emergence of the idea of a special Christian priesthood in place of the Jewish priesthood several major changes of direction had to intervene. First, Christians had to think of themselves as constituting a new religion distinct from Judaism and replacing the Jews of the Synagogue as God's covenanted people.[7]

This was a gradual process. In the Acts of the Apostles we find that the Christians still seem to think of themselves as part of Judaism and even continue to take part in the temple sacrifice and services. The break with Judaism took some years and only came about finally when the temple was destroyed and when the majority of converts were gentiles.

> But there was still a second development before the emergence of the concept of a special Christian priesthood: Christianity had to have a sacrifice at which a priesthood could preside.[8]

This realization also seems to have been gradual. In the New Testament itself we do not find the Eucharist described as a sacrifice, but we do find such references in the writings immediately after the scriptural period. This means also that the ideas of priesthood cannot simply be explained by reference to the texts dealing with the Last Supper. Father Brown concludes:

> The fact that we cannot so simply associate priesthood with the Last Supper context and that we have to understand it as an evolving concept opens us to the understanding that when the Christian priesthood did emerge, it represented more than the heritage of presiding at the Eucharist. The priesthood represents the combination or distillation of several distinct roles and special ministries in the NT Church.[9]

If we say then that the New Testament paradigms for the priesthood involve more than the Last Supper, what are they? Father Brown suggests four basic areas for thought, although there are also others. The four roles that he suggests are those of disciple, apostle, presbyter-bishop, and the celebrant of the Eucharist. Each of these roles involves factors that have been combined into the priesthood as we have it today.

The role of disciple was what helped to shape the spiritual idealism of the Christian priesthood at a later age. The first factor that emerges here is that the disciples were called. From among his followers Jesus chose Twelve who were to be with him in a special way.[10] This call was a demanding one. They were to serve no master other than Jesus, and their vocation was one which allowed of no competition at all. We read, for example, in Luke: "If anyone comes to me without hating his own father and mother and wife and children and brothers and sisters, and his very life too, he cannot be a disciple of mine."[11] It is a background such as this which has led eventually to the ideal of the permanent vocation of the priest. The demands that Jesus made were also put into terms of a life of hardship, with abandonment of possessions and family. This, too, has been drawn into an ideal for the priesthood. It is at this point that we can see the emergence of the ideal of celibacy. Father Brown writes:

> I, for one, think that the Gospel challenge to discipleship is just as relevant today as it was in the 1st century because it touches on the very essence of the generosity demanded of men if they are to be open to God's rule or kingdom. If some of the Gospel demands, such as permanent commitment, seem very difficult to us today, I find no proof that they were not very difficult in the 1st century.[12]

The second role is that of apostle. It is the role that has contributed to our understanding of the priesthood as a ministry of service to others. We find that when the Twelve are sent as Apostles after the resurrection, they are sent to bring the salvation of Jesus to the whole world. The clearest examples of apostle as servant, however, are probably those which are found in the letters of Paul.

Paul understands his function in terms of service. It is, first of all, service to Jesus Christ.[13] It is because he is a servant of

Jesus that he is also a servant of God's people.[14] On this background, Father Brown points out some of those areas of service which are often forgotten. We tend to think of service in terms of friendship or in terms of social services or counselling. Father Brown, however, points out such areas as service of ordinary work. Paul considered himself as serving his people when he worked for his living and was no burden to them.[15] There is also the service of collecting money. This is stressed quite heavily in the Second Epistle to the Corinthians, when Paul speaks with considerable force about the collection and the pledges that had been made for the poor in Jerusalem. There is the service of prayer. Paul refers frequently to the fact of his prayers for those whom he serves.[16] There is the service of suffering. This is probably most evident in the Second Epistle to the Corinthians. It is in his own suffering that Paul finds the sign of his apostolate. For him, his weakness is simply one more sign that the results of his work must come from the power of God. There is, finally, the service of correction. In this Paul is quite strong. Once again in Second Corinthians we can find examples of this, and in the epistle to the Galatians he even refers to them as "fools."[17] But Paul's correction is always an outgrowth of his love for his people, and even the strongest actions, such as excommunications, are tempered by their intended medicinal quality.[18]

The third role is that of presbyter-bishop. The elder or bishop appears frequently in the New Testament. We find references to this office in Acts, in First Peter and in the Pastoral Epistles. The qualities of the presbyter-bishop are described in the Pastorals. The qualities that are described are quite institutional. The presbyter-bishop is expected to be above reproach, temperate, sensible, dignified, hospitable, apt teachers, gentle and not quarrelsome.[19] There are even further stipulations. For example, he cannot be a recent convert nor can he be married twice. As Father Brown points out:

> Here we have an example of the Church setting its own stipulations for its special ministry. Such qualifications would be unintelligible in

a purely charismatic office, but they are quite understandable in a partially charismatic institution established along prudential lines.[20]

The presbyter-bishop is also responsible for correction and censure, but he must be kindly.[21] He also seems to have the duty of caring for finances of the community.[22] At the same time he is seen as a pastor and is described as a shepherd.[23] It is easy to see how an office such as this developed very easily into a structured authority such as we find in the very early Church in the writings of Ignatius of Antioch. Right at the beginnings we find both structure and authority emerging from the New Testament. Father Brown draws these trends together in the following way:

> As a corrective to this development we recall that the various antecedents of the historical priesthood are capable of modifying each other. Precisely because the priesthood is heir to the role of presbyter-bishop, there is a place in the priesthood for a hierarchy of authority, but because the priesthood is heir to the role of disciple of Jesus all authority must be modified by the ideal that one disciple is not to lord it over another or seek the first place in the manner of worldly institutions.[24]

The fourth and final role is that of the one who presides at the Eucharist. The New Testament does not tie the Eucharist directly to the role of disciple, apostle or presbyter-bishop. It is not clear at first who does preside at the Eucharist, nor is it clear just how such people were chosen or appointed to office. The *Didache,* for example, seems to indicate that the Eucharist could be offered by wandering prophets, but it also speaks of bishops and deacons. The growth of the Church, however, and the need for order, soon led to the need to regularize this function also. By the beginning of the Second Century the role of presiding at the Eucharist had been joined to the role of presbyter-bishop. By the end of the Second Century the various roles had been joined to form the Christian priesthood in the essentials that we associate with it today.

I earnestly recommend to the reader that he read Father

Brown's book for himself. The brief outline that I have given here, however, should at least indicate the possibilities that might emerge in regard to diversified ministries for today.

I would like now to turn to the final part of this chapter. This is the area of problems of the ministry, and it may also be that this will give some further insight into the problems of unity and diversity. Once again I shall rely quite heavily on one author. The author is Father Henri Nouwen and the book is called *Intimacy*. My references in particular will be to the chapter entitled "The Priest and His Mental Health."[25] Once again I highly recommend that you read the whole book since it has much to offer for our further understanding of the priesthood.

When a severely disturbed mental patient is admitted to the hospital, the doctor will not simply ask him what the problem is. He will, instead, ask if he knows what day it is, what time it is, where he is, his name, his friends, his job. The doctor is checking to see if the patient knows *when* he is, *where* he is and *who* he is. He is attempting to see the person's orientation in time and space and person. On this basis, Father Nouwen discusses the mental health of the priest in terms of his awareness of time, and self-understanding. He suggests that the priest might sometimes find it difficult to respond to the question: "When, where and who am I?" We can then discuss the priest in terms of healthy timing, healthy spacing and healthy self-understanding.

Healthy timing involves both long-range timing and short-range timing. Long-range timing is the way a priest uses his days, weeks and months in the perspective of an effective life plan. Many a newly-ordained priest leaves the seminary with a "redemption complex." He is determined to save the world, and his time is consumed by meetings, counselling, teaching. It is an endless round and he has no time to withdraw or to think. He is popular because he is available. He cuts down on his sleep, on his reading and on his recreation. After a few years people have still not changed very much. The same problems are there, but they no longer seem challenging. He has seen no new books and has no new ideas. Boredom starts. Lack of sleep causes physical fatigue; lack of motivation causes mental fatigue; lack of inspiration causes spiritual fatigue. There is resignation, irritation and depression. He may stay in the priesthood just to have a home, or he may decide to leave.

The more common affliction, however, is unhealthy short-range timing. This refers to the way in which he uses his hours in one day. He may make no distinction between a time to work and a time to relax. He is always in the rectory, and so always in the work atmosphere. He is usually in the one home, and so his time is ill-defined. There may be a feeling of always being busy and not really working hard or resting well. Work is at random, and he does not know what he will be doing next. He is always at home and never at home. Always at work and never at work. It becomes increasingly hard to distinguish between being busy and being truly useful. Life loses its rhythm, and he becomes the victim rather than the organizer of his time. This would seem to be a problem that is only overcome by his own efforts to organize his time and to make clear distinctions between work and relaxation. The problem is really typical of the man who always complains (or brags) about never taking a vacation, and yet, as far as an impartial observer can tell, he never seems to do any real work either.

Healthy spacing can become a problem for the person who does everything "under one roof." This is a problem in seminaries where all activity—spiritual, academic, social and physical—is under one roof and under one authority. The same may be true of the priest. Everything is done under one authority. The man who suffers some frustration at work can go home to a different situation in the evening. Things that may be frustrating at home can be relieved by a visit to the country club. There are different roofs. But the priest does not always have this kind of outlet. The assistant in the parish may be under the authority of the pastor in regard to his work, but he may also be expected to have his social life with the same pastor, or to recreate with the same pastor. At the same time there are many areas of conduct in which the pastor will expect the assistant to do or not do certain things. There is also the problem of the extent of authority. The priest may have a great deal of delegated responsibility, but little delegated authority. Even those who do have authority are not always clear on the extent of that authority. The assistant does not know what the pastor will think, the pastor does not know what the bishop will think, the bishop does not know what the apostolic delegation will think and the apostolic delegate does not know what Rome will think. Areas of authority are fuzzy. Healthy spacing includes both healthy defining of spaces and healthy defining of responsibilities and authority. The only solution to this would seem to be frank and open discussion with clearly defined limits as the result.

But the basic problem is that of healthy self-understanding. This is the contemporary problem of the identity crisis. If someone's individual identity crisis concerns the basic levels of his personality, he suffers from a severe pathology. He needs psychiatric help. Most people have a rather well guarded hierarchy of relationships with others. Some are nearer, others more distant. If this hierarchy does not exist, the individual may have an individual identity crisis which is not necessarily pathological. This may be the case with the priest. He can easily lose his privacy. He may try to be friendly with everyone and suddenly discover that he really has no friends. He may then ramble about the parish looking for a home. He needs his parishioners more than they need him. He spends much time with them to fulfill his own desires. He cannot be with himself and must always seek others. He may be without spiritual life and without friends and is at a loss. He tries to direct others and finds that he has no one to direct him. The solution here seems to be in our awareness of a need both for priest friends and a spiritual director. Without them we may just wander without knowing who we are.

Apart from such a crisis in individual identity, there may also be the problem of professional identity. Does the priest have a profession? He has had his years of training in theology, but he does not really have someone to direct or criticize his professional competence. A solution for this might be found in a real period of internship for the priest. A period in which he learns, in a supervised atmosphere, to put into practice the theory that he has learned in his years in the seminary. This is something that seems to be coming into existence at the present time, although it is still done at the deacon level. It is something that can enable him to see his own professional competence, just as the period of internship for the doctor enables him to gain the confidence that he needs for his professional competence.

Beyond this question of professional competence, there is also the question of professional reward. A professional man who is hard working and creative receives his reward in praise and increased salary. Many priests do not see the reward of their profession. The reward that is often given is simply silence which indicates that the priest has not done anything wrong enough to attract attention. Another area where reward is often lacking is in the area of professional theological competence. A professional man knows that he must not merely keep informed in his field, but should also make some contributions to it. The doctor or the psychologist spend their lives working with people whom they help, but they also look to make a contribution to their science as a result of their practical activity. Priests may also do the same, but often fail to recognize the opportunities. The very people with whom they work may be the source of their contribution to theology. The fact of the Incarnation makes it possible for us to say that man has become our greatest source of knowledge of God. The parish is as much a field of research for the priest as the hospital is for the doctor. But perhaps the priest will not see this until he has the chance for a real period of internship. The people with whom he comes in contact should be his greatest source of theological insight. Theology is not just an abstract science. It is an effort to understand God and man's relationship to God, and what better place is there to see this relationship than in people? This indicates that the parish priest has missed the boat if he does not see this practical side of theology. He must see the relationship of theory and practice. It also indicates that it might do the theologian some good to have contact with people, and not to spend his time in the ivory tower of a non-person oriented speculation.

1. *Presbyterorum ordinis,* n. 2, translation from: *The Documents of Vatican II,* Walter M. Abbott, ed., Herder and Herder/Association Press, p. 535.
2. *Ibid.,* n. 3, p. 536.
3. *Ibid.,* n. 4, p. 540.
4. *Ibid.,* n. 5, p. 541.
5. Raymond E. Brown, S.S., *Priest and Bishop: Biblical Reflections,* Paulist Press, 1970.
6. Dt 30, 11-14.
7. Brown, *op. cit.,* p. 17.
8. Brown, *op. cit.,* pp. 18-19.
9. Brown, *op. cit.,* p. 20.
10. Cf. Mk 3, 13-19.
11. Lk 14, 26.
12. Brown, *op. cit.,* p. 27.
13. Cf. I Cor 3,5; 15, 10; II or 4,5; Gal 2,20; Phil 3, 12-17.
14. Cf. I Cor 9,19.
15. Cf. II Cor 12, 13-14.
16. Cf. I Thess 1,2; Rom 1,9; Phil 1,4; Phile 4; Col 1,3; Eph 1,16.
17. Gal 3,1.
18. Cf. II Thess 3,14; I Cor 5, 1-5.
19. Cf. I Tim 3, 1-7; Tit 1, 7-9.
20. Brown, *op. cit.,* p. 36.
21. Cf. Tit 1,9-11; II Tim 2,24.
22. Cf. I Tim 3,3-4; I Pet 5,2.
23. Cf. Acts 20, 28-29.
24. Brown, *op. cit.,* p. 39.
25. Henri Nouwen, *Intimacy,* Fides, 1969.

CHAPTER SEVEN:

THE EUCHARIST

WHEN WE SPEAK of revelation we frequently mean that God has revealed certain facts to which we give intellectual assent. However, I find this notion of revelation incomplete and inadequate. If revelation is merely facts, then it becomes quite difficult to explain how it can offer us salvation. It would do nothing other than add to our knowledge, and faith would merely be the admission that these things were so. In the Scriptures it is quite clearly faith that saves men. Saint Paul makes this an essential point, especially in his epistles to the Galatians and the Romans. For Paul revelation is certainly not just a list of facts. It is God's giving of himself to mankind. This giving of God may be expressed in an objective and factual manner, but the facts are not in themselves the revelation even though they are its expression. On the basis of what can be stated about divine and human causality and their relationship to each other, we may state now that God's self-giving changes the person who receives it. In fact, this change of the recipient is the suitable point of reference outside of God which gives meaning to and is, therefore, essential to the existence of revelation. Revelation then involves new power and new life because it is living contact with the living God.

If we see revelation in this way, then Paul's attitude to the sacraments makes more sense. He places special emphasis on the sacraments of baptism and the Eucharist. In the one sacrament we are united with the dead and risen Christ. We share in his re-creation in glory. In the other sacrament we receive the body and blood of the Lord, and in receiving it we are united into his one body. We become one with Jesus and so also we are one with each other.

Paul speaks of the Eucharist in his first epistle to the Corinthians, and he seems to have no intention of proving the real presence of Christ in the sacrament. This he simply presupposes. He is attempting to show that the Eucharist is a basis of Christian unity in Christ and he supposes the real presence of Christ as the foundation of that unity.

The Eucharist is food, but it is a peculiar kind of food. Our offering of bread and wine is transformed into the body and blood of Christ, and it is these which we receive. Usually when we eat food it is assimilated and becomes part of us. We transform the food into ourselves. This is not the case with the Eucharist. Here we eat the body and blood of Christ and it transforms us. We are assimilated by Christ. We become one with him and with each other. We shall consider this unity in more detail in the next chapter, but for the moment I would like simply to pre-suppose that such unity does exist, and to pose some questions about it. When we receive the Eucharist we become one with Christ. Does this really mean anything to us? What does it mean? In its reception do we make any real effort to become more Christ-like? Or does it sometimes become merely a matter of routine? In its reception the person next to you becomes as much a part of Christ as you are and as you hope to be. You therefore become one with each other. Do you treat the person next to you as you would treat Christ? Do you allow the Eucharist to have any in-fluence on your practice of charity toward your neighbor? How can you possibly know that you and he are one and still continue to be annoyed at his faults while you expect him to excuse yours?

In offering the sacrifice of the Mass we are really gathering to re-present the sacrifice of Christ. This offering, however, cannot remain impersonal, as though we could offer Christ without our-selves becoming involved in that offering. We must also be offer-ing ourselves. If we are to live as true human beings and true children of God, then all that we do must be bound up in God. The first element of our sacrifice is that we give ourselves com-pletely to God. This does not mean a merely formal offering of ourselves as we participate in the Mass. It means rather that our offering should be true, complete and internal. Any offering of ourselves should be the continuation of that full and complete offering that was continued in our baptism.

We are not angels, but men with body and soul. This means that our offering cannot be completely internal. It must express itself in the whole man, and so it must have external effects and must be somehow made visible externally. This means that our external acts will be symbolic, but it is by no means an empty symbolism. The symbol does not stand independently but is the expression of a reality in the one who offers the sacrifice. In other words, it is again a question of meaning. We express the true meaning of our internal sacrifice in the form of visible action. We give ourselves, but we do so under the symbol of the gifts that we offer. Sacrifice means that we as individuals offer ourselves totally to God, and that we fully express that offering.

This adds another dimension to the sacrifice. If it is to be total, then it must be social. By reason of our humanity and by reason of our union in Christ, we can no longer live as isolated individuals. We are human beings and Christians with family ties and social bonds. Therefore, we must offer ourselves as we are, as members of the human family. If we do this, then in the offering of ourselves we are also offering all of humanity. But if the whole race is being offered, then the whole race (ideally) should do the offering. Therefore a real sacrifice does not mean mere individual action, but the total offering of humanity in its social nature. Here again this offering must be both internal and external. It is for this reason that certain men are set aside who are appointed for men in the things that pertain to God, that they may offer gifts and sacrifice.[1] This is the basic reason for the priesthood and the reason that the priesthood is a ministry to others.

In view of the social aspect of sacrifice, assembly becomes essential. The sacrifice should not be an act conducted in privacy and apart from the people. While the sacrifice may be a true sacrifice (and have a good deal of social significance) even under those conditions, it is certainly not the ideal. The priest is the servant of the people when he represents them before God in the offering of the sacrifice. In the past there was some discussion of the danger that the priest might turn the sacrifice of the Mass into a private devotion by saying it alone and in Latin. There is a similar danger even now. The danger, however, has tended in the last few years to take a new direction. There is certainly a place in the Church today for experimentation in the liturgy, but this experimentation should be conducted within the proper framework of ecclesiastical authority, so that its beneficial results could be made readily available to all. Unfortunately many seem to have taken experimentation in the wrong way. It is simply not good for priests and small groups to conduct private "experiments" with no intention of producing fruitful results except for some possible effects on the small group involved. While some of the ideas in the underground church may be excellent, the defiance or rejection of authority reduces them to the level of private devotion. They begin to reduce the Mass to "my" Mass. Even this might not be seriously wrong were it not for the fact that this mode of experimentation is frequently destructive of unity and is, therefore, in violation of the basic meaning of the Eucharist in itself. There is the danger that an act which should symbolize unity may be turned into a symbol of defiance and so become hypocrisy. I must also add, of course, that those who exercise authority should not look upon themselves merely as givers of permission. They have the duty of exercising the creative leadership which should promote what is good and new.

The function of worship is really aimed in two directions, at least apparently. From our viewpoint it seems to be directed to God, and yet it is we who change in offering worship. Our worship is intended as an act of homage to God; but this really means that our act of homage is in the offering of ourselves to him. In our worship we recognize his supremacy and make the clear admission that our happiness is to be found in him alone. This in turn leads to prayer of thanksgiving. We recognize that all good comes from God and that we are totally dependent upon him for all that we are and all that we have. This gives rise to prayer of petition, so that even our prayer of petition becomes an act of worship and sacrifice. It is in this full prayer that we express the sacrifice of our own self-sufficiency as we come to realize that without God our efforts are futile.

We must also recognize the fact of sin in the world and in ourselves. In view of this, sacrifice also becomes an act of reparation. In sin we substitute something else for God and break our relationship with him. The sinner must now struggle against this tendency to replace God, and so he approaches God not only as goodness, but as someone whom he has offended by rejecting his friendship. His sacrifice acknowledges sin and he goes to God as to a merciful and forgiving Father. For the sinner sacrifice means an attempt to make satisfaction for what he has done. Of course he cannot simply do this on his own. It can only be accomplished in so far as God accepts his gift of himself. The sinner tries to destroy what he has done and he tries to accept God again as his final goal. This is expressed in his sacrifice by trying to take the gift (which represents himself) and remove it from the world of the profane. In the temple sacrifices this was accomplished by destruction of the gift, but that destruction does not seem to have meant the destruction of the individual. Its destruction was its removal from the profane and its consequent divine acceptance. This signifies God's acceptance of the sinner. In the sacrifice of the Mass there is also removal of the gift (and the offerer) from the world of the profane. Here it is accomplished by means of transformation. The gift becomes Jesus and this real presence of Jesus in the gift is the sign of the transformation of those who offer the gift.

Man offers his worship so that he may become united with God as his creator and his final goal. He enters into the being and life of God. This implies two things. It implies, on the part of God, that he accepts our sacrifices. On the part of man, it signifies that he fully participates in the sacrifice. God's acceptance is shown in the fact that the gifts are set aside as sacred. Man's participation is essential, because the gift is taking his place and is representative of his own internal sacrifice. If man participates even more fully by partaking of the sacrificial offering (for example, in the form of food), then God's acceptance is even more clearly signified, because God now gives himself to man. The altar prepared by man for God becomes the table prepared by God for man.

The Mass is, then, the individual and social offering of man himself under the form of some external gift. Its purpose is to honor God and to make amends for sin, so that man becomes united to God as his creator and final goal. This is what we have in the sacrifice of the Mass.[2] Our gift of bread and wine is offered to God. He perfects this gift by re-presenting the sacrifice of his Son under the appearance of our gifts. He then allows us to participate not only by our internal dispositions and external actions of offering, but also by receiving the victim of that sacrifice as our food.

It is at this point that our sacrifice becomes the sacrament of unity. It is a sacrament of unity with God in Christ, but also of unity with each other. Our own self-giving is united with the giving of all and this is what must have its effect in the rest of our lives.

We can, at times, speak quite glibly of the continuation of the Mass in our daily lives. What we are really saying is that the Mass is the high point of our self-giving. If we do not live truly Christian lives, then our participation in the Mass becomes meaningless. Instead of saying that the Mass must affect the rest of our lives, we might say the same thing in another way. The Mass should be the expression of what we are as Christians. In it we try to sum up what we are and the way that we live. And if our being and lives are not summed up in the Mass, then we are the victims of hypocrisy.

1. Cf. Heb 5,1-2.
2. Cf. Herman A.P. Schmidt, S.J., *Introductio in liturgiam occidentalem,* Rome, 1960, pp. 323-330.

CHAPTER EIGHT:

THE BODY OF CHRIST

THERE WAS A time in the history of theology, from the primitive period to the eucharistic heresies of the early middle ages, when the term "Mystical Body of Christ" had a very full meaning. It was used interchangeably to mean the physical body of Christ as the body of a divine person, the eucharistic body and the body which is the Church. The very fact that the same term could be used of all three gave them a unity which, unfortunately, they have lost somewhat in our own age. While I do not in this chapter intend to reinstate that unity of terminology, I would like to say something about how the three are related as realities. Even though theological exigencies may have necessitated a change in vocabulary, there is no need to allow this to create a separation of ideas which are better understood in unison than when separated.

In the first few of his epistles Paul does not speak at all of the Body of Christ. It is only when he writes his first letter to the Corinthians that he starts to use this image. Probably the idea came to him because of a particular problem in Corinth. The city was at that time notorious as a center of immorality. Paul was anxious to warn his converts against this, but he also wanted to give them solid reasons for his moral exhortations. Moral demands that might have been evident to the Jews were not suited in the same way to the pagan mentality from which the Corinthians had been converted. Paul's line of reasoning was that they were united with Christ and should not be united with sin. He then takes this a step further and says that the man who is united to the Body of Christ is one with him and should not be united with the body of the prostitute. Once he had established this line of thought he could then develop it further. Corinth was also a city of factions.

There had been factions in the various philosophical schools there, and the same thing began to happen in the Christian community. Paul now said that the Christians should not break into factions, because they were united in the one body of Christ. His basic point was unity, and it was only after this that he began to speak of the body as having different parts and the parts as having different functions.

The problem of sexual morality seems to have gone to two extremes. On the one hand there was incest and prostitution, but on the other was a rigorism so excessive as even to hold that sexual intercourse in marriage was sinful.[1] One can readily understand how both extremes had come from one source. The gnostic tendencies of later centuries show a disregard for matter and a concern only for spirit. This tendency was possibly present in the Corinthians too, and Christianity, with its emphasis on other-worldliness, might easily have been mis-interpreted. Where there is total disregard for matter, one of two conclusions follows. One may say that only spirit has value and so what is done by the body is of no consequence. This leads to complete laxism. The other conclusion is that only spirit is good, so one should avoid all material concerns. This leads to rigorism. Paul falls into neither trap, and he is concerned with the whole man, material and spiritual.

This concern is clearly expressed. "The body is not meant for immorality, but for the service of the Lord, and the Lord is for the body to serve."[2] This concept of the body now becomes central as Paul moves on into the notion of the Body of Christ. This development in the first epistle to the Corinthians is occasioned by Paul's attack on immorality and disunity. Yet it is a most important theological concept if we are to learn to look upon revelation as anything more than presentation of facts about God and his plan of salvation. The notions of body, Eucharist, baptism, spirit, unity and revelation make our considerations of the subject so complex that it must be gone into in some detail.[3] The oneness of the Christian with Christ has already been found in the earlier epistles. The Christians are called to share in a glory which is properly that of Christ.[4] They have the Spirit of Christ by which they can call upon God as Father.[5] Christ must be formed in them.[6] By being baptized into union with Christ, they have put on Christ.[7] In the epistle to the Corinthians, this unity takes a new turn as Paul explains that they are one body with Christ.[8]

If we consider the sources of Paul's explanation of Christian unity, we must certainly take into account the corresponding hellenic notion of societal unity as compared to unity "in one body."[9] One of Aesop's fables, concerning the body and its members, had been taken by Menenius Agrippa and applied to the unity of the social order. The notion of this unity seems to have been well enough known that it would not be a matter of surprise to the Corinthians if Paul should also use it. It would certainly not be unexpected when Paul tried to organize the use of charismatic gifts in the liturgical assembly. Yet Paul takes it much further than this. He transfers the whole notion from the realm of simple metaphor to the realm of a mystical reality.

The body of Christ with which Paul presents us is a *physical reality*. Perhaps the best place to begin with an explanation of this is Paul's statement about sexual morality.[10] The body he is talking about here is clearly a physical body. It would seem that he is attacking their apparent disregard for corporeal reality by showing them that this has a very definite place in God's plan for our salvation. The body is meant for service of the Lord.[11] The person who commits sexual sins makes use of his body in giving himself to the sin.[12] The union with the prostitute makes the two one flesh. Here Paul is clearly referring to actual physical bodies, but always with the implied notion of the body as not a mere physical entity removed from the world of the spirit, but a body which is representative of the whole person. This same notion of the reality of the body is expressed again when Paul tells them that their bodies are temples of the Holy Spirit who is within them, which they have received from God.[13] In this statement the metaphor of the temple is based on the reality of the body. The Christian belongs completely to God and so must honor God with his body.[14] The body of man in these passages is clearly his real, physical body. It is an integral part of the whole reality which is man.

There was also a tendency on the part of the Greeks to look upon the soul as being imprisoned in the body, so that salvation might appear to them as the freedom of the soul from bodily dwelling. Paul also rejects this notion as he explains the fact of the final resurrection.[15]

Paul begins his treatment of resurrection with the preaching of the good news. The basic elements of this good news are that Christ really died and rose from the dead, as is attested to by those to whom Christ appeared, including Paul. This is what the apostles preach and this is what the Corinthians have believed. Now, on the basis of the reality of the resurrection of Christ, Paul proceeds to the reality of the eventual resurrection of the Corinthians. It is truly absurd for them to disbelieve in their own resurrection if they accept the resurrection of Christ. And if he has not risen, their faith is in vain. The apostles would in that case have been lying about Christ and about the action of God. Here one might be tempted to think that Paul is pointing to the fact of Christ's resurrection merely as a sign of the truth of what he had preached. In other words, the resurrection would be a miracle meant to confirm the truth of the factual content of the good news of Christ. This view would certainly be minimal and would miss the point of what Paul is actually saying. For him the resurrection is not merely a sign of salvation; it is its cause. Our resurrection will be a *reality because that of Christ is a reality*. Paul is not simply saying that the resurrection of Christ is a sign which confirms the truth of the fact of our resurrection. Christ's resurrection causes ours to exist. Because of their relation to Christ all men will be brought to life again.[16]

In this whole passage on resurrection, Paul has spoken of both Christ and the Christian coming back to life. Now we began on this particular point, in the first place, in order to explain the notion of the body of Christ. Yet Paul has not stated clearly and explicitly that Christ's body did rise from the dead. It is easy to say that he presupposes this, but I think we can say far more than that if we examine what he has to say about the resurrection of the faithful. He sets right out to connect the fact of resurrection with the body. "How do the dead rise? What sort of body will they have when they come back?"[17] It may seem at first that these are two separate questions, the first about the event of the resurrection and the second about the kind of bodies.[18] Yet if we consider the questions and Paul's answer, we see that they are really the same question. The basis of the answer is transformation. The Corinthians have failed to see that the body does not simply die but is transformed. He begins his answer by pointing to the seed which dies so that from it can come a plant. The plant is not the same as the seed, and yet it comes from it. It is somehow contained in it. Again, not all flesh is the same.[19] Men and animals have "flesh" (σάρξ) in common, but it is certainly not the same thing. There is a difference between earthly bodies and heavenly bodies, and so the sun, moon and stars each have a beauty of their own.

On the basis of these analogies the Corinthians are expected to see that there is a vast difference between the body of man now and his body after the resurrection. The body which is sown in decay will arise in incorruption.[20] Its humiliation and weakness are transformed into splendor and strength. The physical body is sown, but a spiritual body rises.[21] The difference between physical (ψυχικόν) and spiritual (πνευματικόν) is practically equivalent to a distinction that we might now put in terms of "natural" and "supernatural."[22] In both instances the common element is the body (σῶμα). In the one case, however, it is the physical (ψυχικόν) body, vivified by the soul (ψυχή); in the other case it is the spiritual (πνεματικόν) body, vivified by the Spirit (πνεῦμα).

It is significant that in this whole passage Paul insists on the humanity of Christ. Jesus is raised from the dead in his full humanity, but in a glorified state. Thus salvation comes not through a spirit but through a whole man. "For since it was through a man that we have death, it is through a man also that we have the raising of the dead."[23] Our relationship to Adam is the cause of our death and our relationship to Christ is the cause of our life. In other words, if we draw out the parallel, we die because Adam died and we rise because Christ rose. In each case the relationship is not simply chronological but causal, and in each case the causality is predicated on a true humanity of both the cause and those affected. Paul explains still further that as the first Adam had become a living creature, so the last Adam has become a life-giving spirit.[24] One author writes:

> Paul compares the creation of mankind in Adam to its re-creation in Christ. The first Adam, as Genesis says, came directly from God and is the source of our natural life; Christ, the second Adam, also came from God and is the source of the new life of glory, for by his resurrection he communicates his glorious life through Adam, and only then the re-creation in Christ.[25]

This re-creation is the transition from our state of human infirmity to a state of risen glory. Neither those in their present state of weakness (flesh and blood) nor the corrupted bodies of the dead can share in God's kingdom. At the last day the corrupt will be recreated in immortality. This is the final victory of Jesus for us all.[26]

In the context of the question of sexual morality, there is no doubt that Paul was speaking of real bodies. As has been shown, in the question of union with prostitutes the bodies referred to are most definitely physical. As a parallel to this, Paul speaks of the body of Christ. The Christians are parts of Christ's body and therefore should not become parts of the prostitute's. The man who has intercourse with a prostitute becomes one body with her.[27] Whoever is united with the Lord is one with him in spirit. If this whole passage is to make sense, then the body of Christ referred to must be his real, physical body. If we do not admit this, then Paul's argument loses all its force. If the union with Christ does not involve his physical body, then the union with the prostitute is of an entirely different order, and Paul's reasoning for sexual morality is meaningless.

The real sacredness of this physical body of man is brought out most clearly in the passages on the resurrection. The body itself is to share in the eternal glory of the Christian. In this context also the body has to be his real, physical body. Here again, to deny this would be to deny the obvious sense of what Paul had said.

The importance of the physical body of Christ is further expressed when Paul turns his attention to the Eucharist. In the passage in which Paul speaks of the institution of the Eucharist, he concludes that anyone who eats the bread or drinks from the cup of the Lord unworthily is guilty of profaning the body and blood of the Lord.[28] Note, first of all, that Paul does not seem to be attempting to prove the real presence of Christ in the Eucharist. This he simply presupposes. He is telling the people of Corinth to recognize the consequences of this belief. In these statements on the profanation of the Eucharist, Paul is not speaking of the body of Christ in the metaphorical sense of a group considered as a body. This is clear in the fact that he is concerned with body and blood. Were he speaking within the limits of the metaphor, we would have no clue as to the significance of the blood. This negative aspect of profanation of the Eucharist is balanced by another viewpoint when Paul speaks more specifically about our sharing or communion in the Eucharistic body and blood of Jesus.[29]

The basis of the Eucharist as a source of unity seems to be the bread itself at first.[30] The supper is called "the breaking of the bread."[31] The notion of unity seems at first to be based on the fact that the bread which is broken remains one loaf ideally. It is the eating of the one food and drinking of the one drink which Paul emphasizes. He points to the exodus as his example. The people ate the one spiritual food (Manna) and drank the one spiritual drink (water from the rock), and still they disappointed God because some of them became idolators.[32] On this basis Paul attacks the notion of participation in pagan sacrifices. Although there are no pagan gods in reality, the heathen sacrifice is a perversion of true religion and so constitutes union with demons rather than with God. It is evident in this whole passage that the source of unity is the common food. Now, on this foundation Paul begins to build a new understanding. The source of unity is transferred from bread to body. Paul writes: "Because there is one loaf, we many as we are, are one body, for we all share the one loaf."[33] Cerfaux writes:

> Saint Paul begins with the identity of the bread and the body, and then goes beyond the usual theme by connecting the notion of unity with the word "body." If the bread is the body, there must be "one body" since there is "one bread."[34]

In this whole study of the body up to this point, we must emphasize again that we have constantly been speaking of the physical body of Christ. Our unity as Christians is in this one body. This implies that we must somehow have contact with this body. The most perfect form of this contact is clearly in the Eucharist. Paul also explains that baptism gives us unity in the same body. He reprimands them for their factionalism by reminding them that their baptism did not consecrate them to him.[35] In the events of the exodus he sees the clouds and sea as a "baptism" which consecrates the Jews to Moses.[36] When Paul comes to speak specifically about the unity of Christians in the multiplicity of the gifts imparted through the one Spirit, he says that we have all been baptized in one spirit into one body.[37] The only meaning that can really be drawn from this is that baptism actually unites us in some way with the physical body of the Christ.[38] If the meaning is merely metaphorical, then the word "body" ($\sigma\tilde{\omega}\mu\alpha$) is used here to mean a collectivity. This cannot be justified from Greek usage at the time of Paul. Even when the word is used in accord with the usage produced by Aesop's fable, its meaning is that of unity rather than collectivity.[39] When, therefore, Paul concludes that we are Christ's body, and individually members of it, he is speaking of the physical body of Christ and is not simply using the word "body" as a metaphor for the Church.[40] This reverses the problem of unity as we usually conceive of it. The problem is not for him how the many can be one, but how the one can be many. His solution is that Christ is one body, and just as one body can be seen to have many members, so too does Christ. The point is not that the members are diverse and therefore are joined into one body. The real point is that there can be diversity without destruction of unity. Paul is showing that the diversity comes from the unity, and not the other way around.[41]

It is this same unity which manifests itself in the Eucharist. In order better to understand the meaning of this unity it might be well to review very briefly the pattern of unity which is found in the Old Testament and which extends to the eucharistic community of the New Testament.

It was in the exodus that the Jews were formed as one people, God's people. They took upon themselves the obligations of the Law as made known to them through Moses, and they ratified their treaty with God in the blood of a sacrifice.[42] Yet even in the exodus and the formation of a new people, it was almost as though God had not yet really committed himself. At least, this commitment was not immediately visible. Even though the Jews were God's people, they were still to spend centuries waiting for God to give them his salvation. They knew that salvation was to come, and gradually they realized that it would come through some individual, but they were never really sure just how or when this would happen. They hoped that it would come through the kings of the davidic line, but this hope was shattered when the house of David fell and was never restored to power. They hoped that it would come through the institution of the priesthood, but this hope also seemed to be gone by the time of Christ. There were some who hoped that it would come through some extraordinary servant of God, but there seemed to be no such servant forthcoming.

While they waited and hoped, they also went astray. In their own actions they revealed the imperfections of their adherence to the covenant. The prophets attempted to recall them, but apparently to no avail. It was then that the prophets began to speak in terms of a new covenant and a new people. Jeremiah said:

> "Behold, days are coming," is the oracle of the Lord, "when I will make a new covenant with the house of Israel and with the house of Judah, not like the covenant which I made with their fathers on the

day that I took them by the hand to lead them out of the land of Egypt
—that covenant of mine which they broke, so that I had to reject them
—but this is the covenant which I will make with the house of Israel
after those days," is the oracle of the Lord: "I will put my law within
them, and will write it on their hearts; and I will be their God, and
they shall be my people. And they shall teach no more everyone his
neighbor, and everyone his brother, saying, 'Know the Lord'; for all
of them shall know me, from the least of them to the greatest of them,"
is the oracle of the Lord, "for I will pardon their guilt, and their sin
I will remember no more."[43]

At the Last Supper Jesus first offered the sacrifice of the
Eucharist. It was offered in terms of "covenant" and "blood." Mat-
thew and Mark speak of "the blood of the covenant."[44] Luke and
Paul speak of a "new covenant in blood."[45] In this supper there
is the joining of the Old Testament themes. The paschal lamb
and the sacrifice are both present. The supper is the paschal
banquet and the sacrifice is clearly indicated, even to the foundation of the covenant in blood. It is parallel to the Passover and
the foundational sacrifice in the events of the exodus in the Old
Testament.

In this case it is the blood of Jesus which is to be sprinkled
on the people. Jesus' notion of himself as Messiah is the answer
to Isaiah's hymns of the servant of God. He is called in justice
and becomes the new covenant of the new people. He is the
light of nations. What Jesus did in the foundation of the Eucharist was to establish a new covenant which replaced the law by
fulfilling it. He founded the new assembly, the new people. God
had now definitively committed himself.

It was on the basis of the formation of the people of Israel in
the exodus that it became necessary for this people to offer sacrifice to the Lord and to honor him by celebrating the banquet of
their deliverance. The same now becomes true of the new covenant. Christ's command to repeat the Eucharist is part of the
foundation of a new people.[46] The blood which is shed for the
many is also commemorated in the banquet which is to be cele-
brated for the many. In the Eucharist is the foundation of the
new people, the foundation of the Church.

The foundation of the Church is not then simply the foundation of a society. It is the foundation of a people. It is the foundation of a people who are united in the continuation of the sacrifice of their saving Lord. The law of this new people is in its heart and not on tablets of stone. It lives in the covenant with God because it is a transformed people.

If we see our adherence to the Church simply as adherence to a hierarchical structure, then we see only the externals. The foundation of the structure and the foundation of the adherence is Christ himself, always present in his Church and always the source of its unity. Our adherence to each is not just the adherence of good will and fellowship. It is the adherence to the one Body of Christ, to the one humanity of Christ in which we have found God, in which we have entered into the life of the Trinity.

It is this unity which is expressed in the Eucharist, and it is a unity which extends to both God and neighbor. It is a unity founded in love. In the first epistle of Saint John we read:

> By this can we be sure that we know him, if we keep his commandments. He who says that he knows him and does not keep his commandments, is a liar and the truth is not in him... He who says that he is in the light, and hates his brother is in darkness still.[47]

> He who has the goods of this world and sees his brother in need and closes his heart to him, how does the love of God abide in him?[48]

> If anyone says, "I love God," and hates his brother, he is a liar. For how can he who does not love his brother whom he sees, love God, whom he does not see? And this commandment we have from him, that he who loves God should love his brother also.[49]

Men are known as lovers of God and disciples of Christ only if they love one another. Their love is a bond of unity. It is a common bond of love which joins us in the body of Christ, and it is this common bond of love which is nourished by the sacrament of the Eucharist.

The Eucharist is, then, not only a sacrifice but also a banquet. It is a meal. Even in an ordinary meal in a family there is a spiritual meaning. It is a concrete expression of the love which binds the family together. It is a manifestation of the work and the love which give life to the members of the family. It is a symbol of family love and unity. So too is the Eucharist.

The spiritual reality which is signified by the Eucharist is the unity of the faithful with Christ and with the members of his Body in the bond of charity.[50] If by communion we were not united to the Body, and so to each other, the sacrament would not have its principal effect.[51] Individual union with Christ would be of little value if we were not by that fact also united with the members of the Body. Christianity is not merely a personal contact with Christ, but it is also an incorporation into the whole Christ. As Saint Paul says:

> The cup of blessing that we bless, is it not the sharing of the blood of Christ? And the bread that we break, is it not the participation of the body of the Lord? Because the bread is one, we though many, are one body, all of us who partake of the one bread.[52]

The sacrament of the Eucharist is a sign which produces that which it signifies. It signifies the unity of the Body of Christ. It is, then, the cause of this unity, and this is precisely why we refer to it as the sacrament of unity. The sign of the sacrament is not simply the bread and wine. The appearances of bread and wine are in themselves symbols, but the real sign is Christ sacramentally present. It is his presence which causes the unity. "The sign of our unity in Christ is the unity of Christ's own body made present at every time and every place in which species are consecrated and received in communion."[53]

It is this which gives justification for the notion that all of the sacraments culminate in the Eucharist. It does not mean that the other sacraments are merely preliminaries to the reception of the Eucharist. It means rather that while in all of the sacraments we are united with Christ, it is only in the Eucharist that we receive the fullness of his charity. Only in the Eucharist are we enabled not only to receive charity directly from Christ, but to rejoice in the life stream of charity which flows through the whole organism from one member to another.[54]

This is why communion is not merely individual union with Christ. "As long as our love for Jesus in the Sacrament of his love is a love only for the Head, without sincere and warm affection for our brothers, without interest in the spiritual and physical needs of his members, our spiritual lives will remain stunted and incomplete."[55] We can never really come to appreciate either the Church or the Eucharist if we never see the connection between them. I would even go so far as to say that we can never appreciate the unity of the divine and human in the person of Jesus if we never see its relationship to the Church and the Eucharist. This is what I meant earlier when I said that it is not we who assimilate the Body of Christ in the Eucharist, but the Body of Christ that assimilates us. We become part of him. We are assimilated into his body.

This opens up a new avenue of thought which I would like to explore later in another chapter. It is this: We speak of the indwelling of the Trinity in man. But do we not really mean that man begins to live in the Trinity? Through the humanity of Christ we have made contact with the divine Persons. Through our transformation as Christians we have entered into the life of the Trinity. Our love and knowledge of God is the divine love and knowledge that God has of himself. We are so totally recreated that we now exist in a completely new order. If we were to attempt to contain the infinite within us, we would only succeed in distorting it. But the infinite can contain us without in any way damaging us. It transforms us into something that we could never accomplish on our own. It is to the completion of this transformation that the Eucharist is leading us.

The greatest of the spiritual writers (e.g., St. Teresa, Meister Eckhart, etc.) seemed to come to the notion that it is we who are assumed by the Trinity and not the Trinity who is assumed by us. This seems to be a common element in the mystics. They realized what had been happening to them. They came to be conscious of God's activity. They realized that as Christians they had been assumed into that activity. This opened them both to

God and to the needs of others. If we are to be real Christians, then we must also realize that mysticism is not a luxury but a necessity. How willing are we to enter into that kind of union in the Trinity? Entrance into it means the total sacrifice of self. How much do we allow our participation in the sacrifice and sacrament of the Eucharist to draw us to that final sacrifice? Entrance into that unity means a total submission of self to the needs of our neighbors. How willing are we to make that submission?

1. Cf. I Cor 7,1-7.
2. I Cor 6,13.
3. Cf. McKenzie, *Dictionary of the Bible*, Milwaukee, 1965, "Body," pp. 100-102; J.A.T. Robinson, *The Body* (No. 5 of *Studies in Biblical Theology*), London, 1963; L. Cerfaux, *The Church in the Theology of Saint Paul*, New York, 1963, pp. 262-286; *The Interpreter's Bible*, Vol. X, New York, 1953, pp. 3-262.
4. II Thess 2,14.
5. Gal 4,6.
6. Gal 4,19.
7. Gal 3,26.
8. Cor 6,12-20; 10,14-22; 11,17-12,31; 15,1.
9. Cf. J.A.T. Robinson, *op. cit.*, p. 59, n. 1.
10. I Cor 6, 12-20.
11. I Cor 6,13.
12. I Cor 6, 18: Note difference between ἁμαρτία and πορνεία.
13. I Cor 6,19.
14. I Cor 6,20.
15. I Cor 15, 1-59.
16. I Cor 15,22.
17. I Cor 15,35.
18. Thus Peifer, *I Corinthians, II Corinthians*, Collegeville, p. 57.
19. I Cor 15,39.
20. I Cor 15,43.
21. I Cor 15,44: σπείρετι σῶμα ψυχικόν, ἐγείρεται σῶμα πνευματικόν.
22. I am here using "natural" to refer to a state of historical nature rather than that of pure nature.
23. I Cor 15,21: δι'ἀνθρώπου in both parts of the verse.
24. I Cor 15,45.
25. Peifer, *op. cit.*, pp. 58-59.

26. I Cor 15,51-58 (cf. vv. 15-26).
27. I Cor 6,16; cf. Gn 2,24.
28. I Cor 11, 23-34.
29. I Cor 10, 14-24.
30. Cf. Cerfaux, *op. cit.*, pp. 263-265.
31. κλασις τοῦ ἀρτομ Cf. I Cor. 10,16: τὸν ἄρτονόν κλῶμεν.
32. I Cor 10, 1-11.
33. I Cor 10,17.
34. Cerfaux, *op. cit.*, p. 265.
35. I Cor 1, 13-17.
36. I Cor 10,2: εἰς τὸ ὄνομα Παύλου ἐβαπτίσθητε.
37. I Cor 12,13: ἐίς τον Μωυσῆν.
38. To say that the meaning of physical body is the only one possible in I Cor 12,13, may seem at first to take too narrow a view of the verse in question. However, this interpretation is based on a number of factors, the first of which is that the whole emphasis on "body" in this epistle has been on "physical body." This in itself would immediately lead us here to say the same thing. Furthermore, if we were to take body (σῶμα) here to refer to the body of Christ in the sense of the body of the Church, then εἰς 'εν σῶμα would mean that we are baptized in order to form one body (Church). In no other case does βαπτίζεσθαι εις have this meaning. For further information on this, you might consult Cerfaux, *op. cit.*, p. 270.
39. For a good explanation of the reasons for accepting the word "body" in terms of "physical body," in spite of the more or less traditional interpretation of it in terms of church, read Cerfaux, *op. cit.*, pp. 272-275, and p. 273, n.24.
40. I Cor 12,12-31; cf. v. 27.
41. Cf. J.A.T. Robinson, *op. cit.*, pp. 58-60.
42. Cf. Ex 24, 1-8.
43. Jer 31,31-34.
44. Mt 26,28; Mk 14,24.
45. Lk 22,20; I Cor 11,25.
46. Lk 22,19; I Cor 11,24-25.
47. I Jo 2,3-4; 2,9.
48. I Jo 3,17.
49. I Jo 4,21.
50. Cf. S.T. III, q. 73, a. 3.
51. Many of the ideas in the remainder of this chapter are based on Thomas Merton's, *The Living Bread*, New York, 1965, pp. 133-139.
52. I Cor 10,16-17.
53. Merton, *op. cit.*, p. 135.
54. Cf. S.T. III, q. 73, a. 4.
55. Merton, *op. cit.*, p. 139.

CHAPTER NINE

PENANCE AND ANOINTING OF THE SICK

IT WOULD SEEM only natural that our attitude to the sacrament of penance will, to a large extent, be determined by our attitude toward sin. Unfortunately there seem to be many people who have the wrong understanding of law and sin, and this leads to similar misunderstandings about the sacrament of penance. One common attitude towards sin would seem to be that there are certain things which are sinful because they have been forbidden by God. If a man chooses to violate God's law he will then be punished for his infraction. In my opinion, this concept of sin is not far removed from a kind of taboo, and it makes God a law-giver instead of a Father. I think that sin is really something quite different, and I will try to illustrate what I mean by means of two examples.

The first of these examples is that of traffic laws. On certain highways you are allowed to travel at sixty miles an hour. If you violate the law and drive at sixty-one miles an hour, then you are technically breaking the law and could be punished for it. But, really, sixty-one is not appreciably more dangerous than sixty. What I'm getting at is simply this: The speed limit is a purely arbitrary figure. A safe speed could be set within certain limits, and the legal speed is chosen from somewhere within that range of possible speeds. Those who make the laws pick some round figure within the limits of safety, and this becomes the legal speed. To violations a punishment is attached. Violations may still be well within the limitations of the safe range, but they are nevertheless violations and are subject to punishment. The law is arbitrary. This is also the way in which some people seem to think of moral law. This is, in my opinion, exactly the wrong attitude.

My second example is the labels on bottles. Suppose that a man buys a bottle of rat poison. It may smell rather pleasant. In fact, it might seem attractive enough to drink. But there on the bottle is a large label on which are a skull and crossbones and the words: "Do not use internally." The manufacturer, it would seem, has placed some restrictions on its use. So the purchaser, being a law-abiding citizen, writes to the company for permission to drink their product. If the company gives the permission and he does drink it, he will still die. The apparent rule in this case was not arbitrary. It was based on the very nature of the relationship between man and the contents of the bottle. Even with permission it is still poison and it still kills the user. This is more nearly what I mean by the moral law or divine law. There are certain things which by their very nature are incompatible with our humanity, and the doing of these things would accomplish our destruction. The Law of God is the warning label. Just as the poison manufacturer's permission would not change the effect of the poison, so God's permission would not change the effect of sin. The difference, however, is that the poison manufacturer, being human, could give the permission. God, being divine, could give no such permission since the granting of it would be contradictory to that truthfulness which is his very being.

The two examples make clear, I think, the notion of moral law which I am proposing. Yet merely to state that this is what I think divine law to be is not sufficient. I would like, therefore, to explain at least briefly why I hold this position on the meaning of law. Let us suppose that the moral law is arbitrary. If this be the case, then any punishment attached to sin is actually extrinsic to the act. In the case of the poison the "punishment" was intrinsic. Use of the poison caused an inevitable result. In the case of the traffic laws punishment is inflicted only if the offender is caught. When he is not caught there is no punishment. God's infliction of such an extrinsic punishment would only be possible if his act followed from ours. But this is impossible. God's acts can in no way depend upon ours, unless we deny his divinity. On the other hand, it is possible to explain sin and punishment if the punishment is intrinsic to sin. The punishment here would be the rejection of transformation. Just as the sin itself would be a negation, so too the punishment would be the same negation. The sin is rejection of God, and the punishment is loss of God. Since God is the ground of our being, what we are really saying is that sin is a self-inflicted attack on what we are. Punishment is the loss of what we are (and so of what we should be). Here again our language leads us to speak of God as punishing the sinner. It is actually the sinner who changes and in so doing punishes himself. In the process of self-creativity we remain free and so we can abuse that freedom. God does not dehumanize us by taking away that freedom, even when we use it against ourselves. Both the sin and the punishment are our choice and are self-inflicted.

Sin is not bad because God forbids it. Rather, God forbids it because it is bad. It is a form of self-destruction. It is a reorientation (or disorientation) of the person. He replaces God with something else. Through sin the individual changes the direction of his life, because he rejects its proper direction, and this is what makes it wrong. In place of God as his goal, he substitutes something less, and so falls short of what he should be. I think that this is what the theologians mean when they speak of sin as turning from God and turning toward creatures.

Sin, therefore, means that which is destructive of the person as a person. A little thought in any area of moral theology will reveal this. For, example, injustice is destructive of persons. A person has both a need and a right to make use of material property in the living out of his life. This need not mean only that property which constitutes the basic essentials of human sustenance. It can also mean that property which is part of a fuller human life involving culture and beauty as human values. For someone, without need and without justification, to take away such property, is ultimately destructive of those values which contribute to the fullness of personhood. Therefore, to say, "Thou shalt not steal," is not merely the statement of legal prescription which forbids something that would otherwise be perfectly all right. It is a statement of something that would in itself be harmful to a person as such. And if one is willing to attack the personhood of another, it is already a sign that he undervalues his own personhood. He is already in that process of spiritual suicide which is sin.

The word "contrition" originally meant something like "breaking a thing up" or "shaking it apart." This is exactly what penance and contrition do. They break down whatever has been put in place of God and allow the penitent to return to God. The guilt of sin is not just something extrinsic added to the sinner as a punishment. And likewise the contrition is not just something extrinisic added to the penitent as a means of escape from his sin. Sin and contrition both imply a real change in the person. Both imply a reorientation of his whole life. This gives real meaning to the theories of fundamental option.

Contrition is really death to self and resurrection in Christ. In this way the sacrament of penance is really very much like the sacrament of baptism. Its reception is the external sign of what happens to the penitent. We might also draw a parallel between baptism of desire and perfect contrition without the sacrament of penance. In both cases there has been an internal change in the individual, but mere internal response is not sufficient, just as mere internal worship is not sufficient. The whole man must be involved in every instance. If a man worships God internally he will find it impossible to avoid external signs of worship. He will at least begin to make changes in the way that he lives. The man who truly has the desire of baptism will find it impossible to keep that desire locked within him. Even if he does not know what baptism is, he will begin to change the way that he lives. If he knows what baptism is he will not be able to live with himself without receiving it. The sinner who is truly contrite will find that he cannot keep that contrition completely within him. His life will also begin to change externally. He will turn to God and begin to do his best to avoid whatever has caused the sin. If he knows that the sacrament of penance is necessary, then he will not be able to live with himself in good conscience without receiving it. Just as the Church is the external sign of God's presence in the world, and just as baptism is the external sign of one's entrance into that Church, so also the sacrament of penance is the external sign of one's reconciliation in the Church. None of these signs are mere symbols. They are signs which accomplish what they signify, because they are the finalization of the change in the individual. They are not merely external signs. They might be better described as external realities corresponding to internal realities. They are the official ecclesial completion and ratification of transformation which has already begun within the individual. This is why the sacraments are not magic. In order to produce their intended change, the person who receives them must be moved internally by grace.

The sacrament of penance has a definite communitarian aspect. I have mentioned that God makes his presence in the world visible in that community which constitutes his people, the community which assumes its greatest visibility in the Church and also its only complete form. But to speak of God's people is to speak of a gathering of persons united with God and with each other. Each of these persons is an individual different in many ways from any other individual. Each of us, therefore, reveals some aspect of God in his own way. To fail in this revelation is not merely something that affects us independently of our relationship to the others. If in our lives we fail to reveal God properly, then we fail ourselves, but we also fail God and his people. If sin is destructive of ourselves, it is also destructive of our capacity to reveal God. But this is a function that we have as members of a community. Therefore, sin, even the most secret sin, is really an offense against the whole community. It is not enough, then, to speak of individual reconciliations with God, as though holiness were merely "my" holiness. The sinner must also be reconciled with the community. This is the reason for the necessity of an act of penance before the whole community. This has assumed the form of an act of reconciliation before the priest who acts in the name of the community. The private form that the sacrament of penance has assumed has, of course, resulted in some loss of consciousness of this communitarian element. Such things as penance services may, perhaps, be one way in which we can begin to regain this consciousness. At the same time, an increased awareness of the real malice of sin can also help us to see the proper place of the community.

In a way, the sacrament of anointing of the sick is very much like penance. It also is a kind of contrition. It is a sort of breaking up of something within the recipient. The person who is in danger of death must still prepare himself for it. He is torn between two attractions. On the one hand, there is the fact that he is a Christian and has spent his life waiting for this moment. His whole life has been a preparation for the completion of his unity with God in Christ. He became a Christian in order to enter into that unity. He lived as a Christian in order to maintain that unity. Now he is going to die as a Christian in order to complete that unity. On the other hand, he is a man who has lived in the world. He is a man attached to family and friends. He is a man for whom spiritual realities are ultimate, but for whom material realities are visible. In spite of his desire for the completion of his unity with God, he will still find it hard to separate himself from the world. He will be in a quandary—wanting death and not wanting it; wanting life and not wanting it. It is this conflict which must be broken up in his final contrition. This is what is accomplished in the sacrament of the anointing of the sick. It is a sacrament which brings him internal peace and prepares him for his final peace in God.

At times the change which takes place in this sacrament is quite visible. Any priest who has administered the sacrament has seen this happen at some time. A person may very well be almost at the point of despair. He is fearful of death and yet has given up the hope of life. He receives the sacrament and becomes a new man. He is now happy and ready to do God's will, whether this means living or dying. I have myself seen this change occur so visibly that it was unmistakable. On the surface it is a transformation which is not difficult to explain. It may be psychological. In fact, I would say that it is. But does this mean that it is not sacramental? I do not think so.

In all of us there should be a real spirit of penance. All of us are sinners and should be aware of our sinfulness, and this creates in us the spirit of penance. This does not mean that we spend our lives making our neighbors unhappy by constantly bemoaning our own unworthiness. A true spirit of penance is a spirit of happiness. We derive joy from the fact that we have been changed by God. We are happy that in spite of our sins he has chosen to accept us. He has recalled us to himself. A spirit of penance is not a spirit of fear but one of joy. If we have true penance, then we will also practice penitential acts, but again these acts will be such as are destructive of our own bad attachments. They are not destructive of the happiness of our friends.

True penance will not simply rely on the efficacy of human penitential acts. It will also mean humble confession of sins with the awareness that this humble confession before God is the means of your forgiveness. Conversion to God removes sin and guilt. If we truly believe this, then our conversion to God is a source of the greatest joy. If we truly believe it, then we will try to draw others to penance, not by creating in them a horrible fear of divine punishment, but by creating in them a love of divine goodness.

CHAPTER TEN

CONFESSOR AND PENITENT

THIS CHAPTER WILL concentrate primarily on the place of the priest in the confessional. My intention, however, is not that this should be a chapter for priests which the lay reader may omit. What I will say to priests I also mean to be said for penitents. In the selection of a priest for confession the penitent should be aware of the qualities demanded of a good confessor and should seek out a man who has them (or, at least, one who really tries to have them).

Sanctification is to be found in our union with Christ. This does not mean a passive kind of union between me and God without regard for others. It does not mean an inactive union in which we merely receive. It is a union in which we become so much one with God that we begin to care for others as we know that he cares for us. It is this care of God for us that gives us our internal peace in spite of all our human faults. It is our exercise of this same care that can bring peace to others. They are to find God in us just as we see Christ in them. Each Christian must be the source of comfort for others. And if this is true anywhere, it is certainly true in the confessional.

There has been much discussion in the past few years on the possibility of general absolution as the normal practice. One of the central points at issue here has been the difficulties of confessing to a priest. There can be no doubt that it is difficult to go to someone and tell him that you have committed sins—sins for which you are sorry and of which you are ashamed. But what really makes it difficult? There is, of course, the difficulty created by one's own pride (and I mean just normal human pride, not anything sinful in itself). Unfortunately, however, it is often the priest himself who is the source of the problem. He may listen half-heartedly and give no advice beyond the recitation of a few Hail Mary's. And what good does that do? Or he may listen attentively and then humiliate the penitent to the point of tears by telling him what a horrible sinner he is. And what good does that do? It may turn the penitent away from confession for the rest of his life.

In great measure the confessor is the one who determines what confession is to be. He can make it a lifeless recitation of a list of sins without any help for the person who would desperately like to avoid these sins in the future but doesn't know where to begin. Confession can easily become just such a list if the confessor takes no time to understand the penitent and is satisfied with a rather mechanical assignment of a penance. On the other hand, the confessor can also make confession a trial by fire, a time of terror, a tasteless and terrible ordeal that no one but a saint could endure. Yet frequently enough the penitent is there precisely because he is not a saint. The result may be fear of confession which makes it an impossibility. Or the confessor can make confession something good, even when it is not especially easy. He can make it a time when the penitent has the chance to express his sorrow, to make his effort to change, to ask for advice, to find that he has a friend who will not only listen and try to help, but who even has the power to forgive. This is the reason for confession of sins to a priest. It makes no sense that there should be a list of sins simply in order to have a list. It must have some further purpose. The purpose is the benefit of the penitent. No one who uses his common sense would hold that the priest has ready answers for every problem. He is not a computer who returns programmed responses to predetermined questions. But he is a man who should be willing to listen to others and to help them work out solutions to their problems. (Obviously I am not here speaking of those whose problems demand other types of professional help. In these cases the confessor should have the sense to send them to someone who can offer the help they need.) If the priest has no idea of the problems of the penitent he cannot be of very much help to him. If he does not know what the sins are, or with what frequency they occur, then he does not really understand the penitent's problems. While it may at times seem that general absolution would make things easier, who would reap the benefit in the generality of cases? Would it be the penitent who would now have to try to help himself? Or would it be the confessor, who would now have a lot more time? Time for what? For himself or for others? The purpose of listing sins and the number of times that they have been committed is not some legalistic purpose determined and imposed by canon law. Its purpose is to give the sinner a chance to express his sorrow and the confessor a chance to be of some assistance.

I think that the greatest virtues of a good confessor are patience and kindness. A priest may hear confessions for hours at a time. He may be ready to fall asleep. He may be dying for a smoke. He may have a headache. He may just be bored. Yet for the penitent who kneels before him, this is an important moment. For him it is the only confession that day. It may be the only one for the last twenty years. And the priest's sleep or cigarette or headache or boredom might easily turn him away for another twenty. He may be halting and stumbling over something that the confessor could say for him in half the time. Yet the priest must be patient and not interrupt. He may be describing a problem and it must be heard through to the end so that he may at least have the assurance that he has been heard and understood. He may be a bit frightened and tongue-tied and he must be calmed down and put at ease. Lack of patience might contribute to the destruction of his life. At the moment of confession it is the confessor who is the penitent's contact with the loving mercy of the Father, and he must see in the confessor a divine patience.

Kindness in the confessional can mean a number of things. Still I think that real kindness can be determined best if the confessor should act forgivingly. The person comes to confession because he is sorry and seeks forgiveness. In his actions the confessor should make it clear that this sorrow is accepted and that God's forgiveness is being granted. It is in such human acts that the revelation of God is made present in the world. A priest who sounds as though he doesn't care or who sounds as though he is annoyed at what the penitent has done is certainly not being kind.

There are also times when being kind means being firm with a penitent. This should, however, be the kindness that one might expect from a loving father. I almost hesitate to use the term "father" because there seems to be an attitude at present, even among priests, that this means paternalism in the Church. There is a world of difference between fatherliness and paternalism. Paternalism is a perversion of fatherliness. It treats others as unthinking children and tries to stop them from taking responsibility. This is not what the confessor should do. Real fatherliness is an active concern for the penitent. It tries to develop him. It attempts to lead him to responsibility and to the state where he makes his own judgements and decisions. But it also realizes that responsibility depends upon formation, and so the confessor who is fatherly will also do his best to assist the penitent in the proper formation of conscience.

The priest who ignores sin in a penitent is not really being kind to him. What I mean is that the confessor assumes some responsibility to the penitent in the area of teaching him. To ignore this responsibility to his penitent is to be uncharitable to him. For example, the adolescent who is involved in a habit of masturbation should be brought to the point of being able to see that what he is doing is wrong. This does not mean that he is simply to be told that it is an action that is objectively sinful. Rather, sufficient explanations should be given, as often as necessary, to bring him to the point at which he sees what is wrong and begins to control it because it is now his decision to do so. It is certainly no favor to him simply to tell him that the problem is psychological and therefore not culpable. While this may alleviate his pangs of conscience, it does not solve his problem and it offers him no spiritual assistance. The real problem may well be that the adolescent is in a process of growth and that the masturbation may be a symptom of the fact that he is arriving at maturity. He is passing out of the stage of the selfishness that is there to a great extent in childhood, and into a stage of adult openness to others. Sexuality is part of this adult openness, but the adolescent is only now beginning to cope with it. His emotional responses may still have to outgrow childhood, while his physical responses have already done so. He is at a stage of the assumption of self-responsibility that manifests itself at one level in a kind of rebelliousness and at another level in terms of masturbation. Thus, while the priest realizes that there may not be any real sin involved, he should also realize that there are now great opportunities for growth and the ability to control the tendency to masturbate may be a sign that such growth is actually occurring. He might, therefore, approach the problem from the viewpoint of helping the adolescent to a new stage of openness to others and be able to assist his overcoming the masturbation without concentrating the penitent's attention on it as though it were the real problem. This type of assistance demands that the penitent feel free to make use of the confessor's time and that the confessor be willing to understand his penitent and to help him develop. Dismissing the problem as "not sinful" would not have been the solution. The confessor should also understand that the same problem in an adult may be symptomatic of something deeper and that in some cases it might even demand some further professional assistance.

Kindness also means treating individuals as individuals. It means listening to their problems and making a real effort to help them find solutions which will work in their particular circumstances. It means that penances are not to be assigned mechanically. It means that the penitent should be encouraged to return so that the confessor may ascertain the validity of any advice that had been given.

Kindness is not only applicable to those who have been away for a long time, or to those who commit serious sins, or to those who have habits of sin. It is equally applicable to those persons who really do live holy lives and who are not committing serious sins. These are the people who make confessions of devotion. They try to make frequent use of the sacrament, even though there is

no absolute necessity of its reception. In these instances the penitent should be encouraged to make his confessions thoughtfully.
Sometimes it may happen that the confession has become rep-
etitious. The same sins are repeated time after time. Examina-
tion of conscience has become routine. The repetition of the same
confession has made it mechanical. The penitent may feel that
nothing is changing in his life. There is no sign of further progress. When he reaches that point he may feel that confession has
no more meaning for him, and he may even stop receiving the
sacrament of penance. He starts to drift and it gradually becomes
increasingly more difficult to return. The confessor can help here
by teaching him that confession should not be the repetition of a
list. His confession does not involve serious matters and he has no
need to recall a complete list with exact enumerations. He need
not repeat the same things time after time. I am certainly not advocating that he should introduce more originality into his sinning.
What I am advocating is that his use of confession should be more
thoughtful. He should begin at first to concentrate on those areas
where there is true sorrow. He may have been uncharitable in
minor matters hundreds of times, but the purpose of his confession is not to break already established records. It may happen
that on five of those occasions he really did feel sorrow and really
is determined not to allow this to happen again. These are the
instances that he ought to confess. This will have a gradual but
very real effect on every area of his life.

   The priest and penitent should also make use of the confessional for spiritual direction. While this is certainly not the
ideal for direction, for some people it is the only direction that
they will get. I will return to the question of spiritual direction
in the twelfth chapter, but for the moment I would like to point
out that the confessor should at least take the time to determine
the state of the penitent's prayer life and of the frequency and
meaningfulness of his reception of the sacraments. Further direction in both areas can be accomplished gradually and in a very
non-technical way.

   To summarize: Kindness means that you are willing to assume

responsibility for the spiritual welfare of others. This is true in the relationship between confessor and penitent. It means taking the time and trouble to be of some real assistance to others.

Most of what I have said of penitents can also be applied in general to the care of the sick. They need help and encouragement and the Christian has the obligation to see that they get it. In this the priest plays an important part. The preparation for Christian life and Christian death are really the same preparation.

Both the administration and the reception of the sacrament of penance are serious responsibilities in the Christian life. The sacrament should be as fruitful as possible both for confessor and penitent. Whether you receive it or administer it, it is part of that active and vital union with God which is your sanctification.

CHAPTER ELEVEN

PAIN AND DEATH

I SUPPOSE THE worst thing about pain and death is the fact that they can seem so unreasonable. Or perhaps unreasonable is not really the right word. It is not that we cannot find any reason for them, it is more that they tax our reason to its limits. They lead us beyond reason into the realm of faith. But the very fact that they lead us into the realm of faith can help us to understand their reason for existence.

We can, of course, explain pain and death as punishment for sin. In this sense they are burdens to be borne because of our own rejections of God in so many ways. But this explanation is never truly sufficient. We are still left with a problem which seems at times to defy our understanding. What of the suffering of the good? If it were only the bad who suffered, then we could, perhaps, accept pain and death. But it is never only the bad who are faced with them. To some extent all men must suffer; all without exception must die. It is often those who seem best of all who suffer the most. For this reason I do not think that we can fully explain pain and death as punishments. This is not to say that we cannot explain them as the results of sin. They can be the results of sin without being in themselves a punishment for each individual. Jesus himself did not escape them.

We might begin to find a better understanding of the problem of pain if we were to look upon it more from the viewpoint of purification or transformation. One of the results of sin in the world is obscurity. By this I mean that sin in the world makes it harder to see the presence of God. The man who lives a truly good life can overcome that obscurity to a certain extent. He can begin to see God's goodness as it is manifest in himself and in those around him. He can see the good of this world in the love of family and friends. But this good can also hold him down. It can make it all the more difficult to realize that even this good is only a shadow of what is yet to come. It is no more than a pale reflection of the final happiness that God has prepared for those who love him. It is death which separates us from this world and brings us to that final happiness. It is pain which helps to transform us.

Pain separates a person from everything around him. It stops his enjoyment of this world. It counteracts the pleasure which holds him here. It separates him from others, from family and friends. When pain becomes truly great it can even separate him from himself to some extent. It makes him conscious of his own weakness. It makes him conscious of his own lack of ability to control his environment. The person who is rejected by others finds this awareness through spiritual suffering. The man who is surrounded by loving family and friends finds the same awareness in physical pain. It is at this point that his faith must take over. He is now separated from the love of self and the love of others. But separation opens him to the love of God. He must depend totally on the goodness of God. If he can recognize that this pain is a way of entrance into God's love, then he has found the reason for pain. But it is a reason that goes beyond the limits of simply human reason. It is the reason of faith. It is an awareness that can only be his if he is willing to immerse himself in that transformation which is effected in his first love of God. For the Christian, then, pain is understandable only because of what has happened in baptism. The Christian entered into the death of Christ in order to be able to enter into his resurrection as well. The person who has lived his baptism all his life will also be prepared for this final ordeal. All the small separations from the world have prepared him for this great separation. And just as all the small separations may be accompanied by small pains, so this great separation may be accompanied by great pain.

Part of the pain of this kind of suffering is also the fact that it is then that God seems far away. We can ask for release from the pain, and find that our prayers are not answered. Just when we seem to need God's mercy most, he seems most deaf to our pleas. The problem is, perhaps, that at this point God's goodness does not appear to us as it really is. He is separating us from anything that can stand between us and him, and our prayers for release from this process are not going to be heard in the way in which we might like them heard. C.S. Lewis, in writing of his grief at the loss of his wife, said: "The terrible thing is that a perfectly good God is in this matter hardly less formidable than a Cosmic Sadist. The more we believe that God hurts only to heal, the less we can believe that there is any use in begging for tenderness. A cruel man might be bribed—might grow tired of his vile sport—might have a temporary fit of mercy, as alcoholics have fits of sobriety. But suppose that what you are up against is a surgeon whose intentions are wholly good. The kinder and more conscientious he is, the more inexorably he will go on cutting. If he yielded to your entreaties, if he stopped before the operation was complete, all the pain up to that point would have been useless. But is it credible that such extremities of torture should be necessary for us? Well, take your choice. The tortures occur. If they are unnecessary, then there is no God or a bad one. If there is a good God, then these tortures are necessary. For no even moderately good Being could possibly inflict or permit them if they weren't."[1]

We are called to share in the life and goodness of God, and we might expect this process to be painful. We are finite creatures who must undergo a profound change in order to share in the glory that is to be ours. For us God's goodness makes him all the more awesome, until we can be separated from ourselves and be with him completely. It is only then that we can find ourselves as we are intended to be.

Our separation from self and world finally comes in death. But death is by no means the end. It is, rather, the opening to the fullness of life in God. The Christian who lives out the death and resurrection of Christ from the time of his baptism is in constant process of approaching this fullness. His death is not a mere emptying out of himself, for in it he receives himself back in his final completion as a child of God. In this sense it is almost as though the real Christian is so filled with the life of God that his earthly existence is no longer capable of supporting this fullness. He must simply begin to exist in a new way.

The best way to explain what I mean is, perhaps, by means of an analogy, but a good analogy is difficult to find. The best one that I could think of was that of a man swimming under water. When you swim in clear, tropical water and see the plants and animals around you in the blue, water-filtered sunlight, you are surrounded by beauty. For a fish, this is the whole world, and, if the fish were capable of thought, he would be amazed by the beauty that is his world. Man can look at it and enjoy it, but he is also aware constantly that this is not his whole world. He must make use of all sorts of artificial devices to remain there for any length of time. For man this is merely one part of the world. He is capable of setting aside his devices and emerging into the clear light of the sun. He can see that the beauty of the underwater world is a kind of reflection of what is above the water. It is a beauty in which movement is more difficult than it is in the air. The fish can't live outside of the water, and for him the air means death. But man is meant for more than the fish, and for him the world outside the water is his real home. It is almost as though death is our emergence from the water that surrounds us. We live a life in which we can find love and goodness and beauty all around us. Yet we are not meant only for this life. We are drawn to our real home, which is in the life of God. The swimmer finds it painful to have to leave the splendor of the sea, because he leaves behind him a world which is magnificent. The man who dies also finds it difficult to leave the world in which he has lived for so long, but it is only by leaving it that he can enter into his real life. He too must set aside his devices and emerge from the reflected glory of God into its full light. "There are things which no eye ever saw and no ear ever heard, and never occurred to the human mind, which God has provided for those who love him."[2]

The swimmer is so filled with a fuller life, that the life under water could not long sustain his existence in its fullness. The Christian is so filled with life that he must eventually leave this world, since it can no longer sustain his fullness.

For the family and friends of the person who dies, there is also a time of suffering and trial, but it is a suffering different from the pain that recalls the dying person. It is a pain of separation and a feeling of helplessness in the face of agony. It is the pain of having to relinquish someone who is loved. We must, however, admit that there is a certain degree of selfishness in this pain. Perhaps selfishness is too strong a word. I do not mean to imply in any way that this feeling is for the Christian something sinful. It is the pain that comes from not having someone good here any longer. It is the trial of no longer being able to share our joys with someone who has shared them so often and so well. We can no longer look to him for advice and consolation and the participation in our happiness. In losing a friend we also lose something of ourselves. Even our joys are different, for we no longer see their reflection in him. Yet, since all our joys in this life are themselves a reflection of a far greater joy that we are meant to share, we are the ones who remain in the reflection while he has now begun to live in the reality.

Every parent who really cares about his children must look forward to a very painful parting. The time will come when the child must be set free. He must find his own way and must live his own life. Real parental love is capable of this sacrifice. True love never captures a person and holds on to him. It never suffocates the loved one. It gives without asking to receive, although it always finds great happiness in receiving of and from the other. True love must be liberating. A parent must dedicate himself to the welfare of his child, but he must also realize that the child is in process of growing into maturity. He cannot always remain a child. When his adulthood comes, he must be ready to stand on his own and be himself. In order to do this he must be free of his parents. To offset the pain of setting the child free, the parent has the consolation of seeing him exercise his freedom in the best possible way. This capacity is the result of all that his parents have done for him as he grew up.

This same kind of freeing process must be a part of all human love, if it be true love. Husband and wife must love each other in such a way as to free each other completely. Each must see that the other becomes all that he can be, without ever becoming a possession. This same element of freedom must exist in the love of families and friends. It is a love that overcomes the temptation of selfishness. It is a love that wants to share. It is a love which desires only that the other person be all that he can be. But this kind of love must always involve pain, because it always involves loss of possession. When a person dies we must also be prepared to set him free. He is on his way to final completion, and we cannot stand in the way or try to hold on to a selfish love. Our grief will always have its consolation. We have lost possession of someone only to see him gain possession of himself in God. We have allowed him to be free to be what he was always meant to be.

Pain and death are unreasonable only to a faithless person. Even to the man of faith they tax his reason to its limits, but his understanding is not tied down to the small limits of reason. He is opened to God, and in this openness he can see the real meaning of events. Pain and death draw him to see the world and himself as they should be seen. They constantly remind him not to mistake the reflection for the reality. The man who has no faith is like a fish who sees the swimmer leave the water and is certain that he is leaving all that is beautiful and good. He will act as though the only result of death is annihilation. The fish would think only in terms of his own limited existence, and could not possibly understand another, at least he could not understand it without a transformation that would probably be painful to him. The man of faith knows that leaving this life is not at all the end. It is the beginning. Death is merely our leaving the land of reflected light and our entrance into the direct light of a new world. It is a world for which we still prepare and into which the dead person has preceded us. He will wait for us there until God shows us the proper place at which we too may emerge into the open air.

1. C.S. Lewis, *A Grief Observed*, Seabury Press, New York, 1961, pp. 35-36.
2. I Cor 2,9.

CHAPTER TWELVE

SPIRITUAL DIRECTION

NO FULLY DETAILED analysis of spiritual direction is really possible, since practical points can be determined only by the factors of personality, circumstances, abilities and needs of the director, the one who is directed and the relationship which exists between the two. There are, however, some points of general information which can be presented schematically.

From what has been said above, it follows that the person who makes real use of confession will have a regular confessor. This is not the same as having a spiritual director. One may have a regular confessor with whom he discusses those areas of his life in which there is sin or the danger of sin. Spiritual direction implies something more positive, since the director is concerned not only with sin but with the more extensive questions of prayer and general spiritual formation.

There are certain things that a director is not and should not be. He is not a question box into which one can place problems demanding canned solutions. Ultimately, it falls upon each person himself to find his own solutions to his own problems. He may find discussion helpful in arriving at a solution, but it is he who must arrive at it. The director is not a refuge from the harsh realities of life. If the director becomes any of these things, then paternalism has begun to raise its ugly head. The individual is finding it possible to shirk the task of assuming responsibility. He has placed his own responsibility in someone else. Quite apart from the spiritual implications of such a situation, it would even seem to be detrimental to the mental health of the individual involved. Overdependence is damaging to the personality of the individual, and is therefore damaging to his spiritual development.

Certain attitudes in the relationship of director and the one directed can also be detrimental. For example, the one who seeks direction may do so without really being sure what he needs or what he hopes to achieve. He may feel that he must visit the director regularly, but really has nothing to say. He may feel that each visit demands some specific and important problem; but his own problems at the time seem rather petty (or, if not petty, at least commonplace). He therefore sets up a straw man for the director to knock down. While the results of this may be consoling in that they have at least indicated the ability of the director to produce arguments, they are of no real help to the questioner. They were not his problems.

Related to this may be the fact that the person finds it a problem to be completely open with the director. Openness, however, will come only in time and with mutual trust. There may be need of a period of only tentative trust in order to establish a real relationship with the director.

The individual who seeks direction may also be guilty of lack of thought. By this I mean basically that he may not really know himself and he has never taken the time and effort to do so. He may even be aware of problems and may have arrived at workable solutions (perhaps solutions that the director has suggested), but they have not been put into effect. He has not really thought out the problem, the solution, or the relationship between the two. The solution remains valid but ineffective.

Another detrimental attitude is fear. If there is real fear of the director, then a change in directors is indicated. There should be a basis of friendship. But even where this exists, there may remain the fear of human respect. There is fear that full revelation of oneself may result in loss of respect or friendship. This is only overcome in time and with the gradual realization that if the director is really a friend and does really have a Christian love for the individual, then nothing is going to break that bond. Any self-revelation of faults, no matter how secret, will be one more means of cementing the friendship. No director who is really doing his job is going to be shocked or repelled by a revelation made in humility and sincerity. It creates a closer bond and allows the direction to be more effective.

Detrimental attitudes may also be found in the director. He may talk too much and not listen enough. This creates the risk of his never really knowing the person to whom he is giving direction. This could cause real damage and be of no assistance at all. As director it is essential that he know the other person as well as the person knows himself. This is accomplished only by listening.

Also, if the director does not know the person he may run the risk of abstractionism. By this I mean that he may make applications of abstract principles without being sure of their concrete application. A perfect (and disastrous) example of this is the director who moves someone toward a life of celibacy because he (the director) considers this to be, in the abstract, a higher calling. If he had gotten to know the person he might have found that the best way for him to truly express his Christian love was by centering it in one person in marriage.

There is also the danger of over-direction. This happens when the individual allows the director to assume full responsibility for his actions. The director may be too authoritative in his direction, or he may unwittingly fall victim to a lack of strength in the one who is directed. If the director is too authoritative, it might be well to change directors. If the director is victimized by the other person's lack of strength, it may be that he does not know him well enough. In either case there is the danger of over-direction which will introduce paternalism. This would harm the individual by leading him away from rather than in the direction of responsibility.

A related danger is that the director may try to impose his own spirituality on the other person. By this I mean that the director's life may have a certain pattern which has proven helpful and profitable in his development. He then takes it for granted that an identical pattern will work for others. There is an implicit effort to make over the individual in a new pattern, but it may be a pattern that he cannot fit. Instead, the director should make every effort to know those who come to him, and to know them as individuals with widely varying personalities and needs. Each should develop from within and along lines which allow greatest development of personal potential.

Finally, I would point to the danger of under-direction. This happens either when the director does not care about the other person or is too eager simply to agree with the other person's point of view. Simple agreement in every instance as a matter of policy is not direction. It offers the other person nothing. He is simply being left to himself with the somewhat dubious comfort of an echo to keep him company.

It should also be noted that direction should involve a definite structure. It should be structured in that the director tries to determine those areas in which the person actually does need assistance and that he directs his advice to those areas. It must not become random or haphazard discussion of generalities. It must also be structured in terms of time. Interviews that have no end in sight tend to degenerate into bull sessions that can defeat the purposes of real direction. Lack of structures can also contribute to the destruction of a situation in which direction is possible. They can lead too easily into a kind of relationship which becomes too "personal" and in which emotional involvement of the director renders him incapable of the kind of objectivity that must be present if he is to be effective.

We may now turn to a consideration of proper attitudes. Some elements of relationship between the director and the one who is directed take some time to develop. The person who seeks direction should feel comfortable with the director. He should feel free enough to be open and completely honest. This may be a gradual process and should not be forced. Personal revelation is really possible only with friends, and friendship develops gradually. The fear of loss of the respect of the director is overcome only as the individual comes to realize that there is present a real friendship which will not be disturbed by problems. Love and respect will be increased in proportion to openness, provided only that the director is truly Christian. We should also be aware that this friendship must maintain itself at the professional level of direction. It must not become simply emotional involvement.

Anyone who seeks direction must make the personal effort to understand himself. This does not mean that he must seek out every hidden fault and lay it before the director. He must also understand his good points. He must know himself as he is. This means that, while he should be aware of his shortcomings, he should also be aware of the fact of his own Christian transformation and dignity. He should begin to see his good qualities as being in themselves revelatory of God's goodness. He is the revelation of God, and his effects at progress are not efforts to destroy some monster. They are efforts to make the revelation of God in him as clear as possible. As he realizes this his motivation will be properly formed; and formation of motivation is essential. It is on this ground that he is going to be able to assume full responsibility.

He must at the same time realize that he is human and that there will be a necessary limitation on his efforts. Failings should be the source of neither discouragement nor shame, but the source of a greater reliance on God's goodness. This reliance should be accompanied by the realization that God has called us as we are—human and weak and prone to error. This leads to the realization that effort is more efficacious than complete success.

On his part, the spiritual director must make efforts, especially in the initial stages, to put the individual at ease. The atmosphere should be relaxed and conducive to conversation. It is only in such a situation that the person will really find it possible to be open. The director must also be a good listener. By this I do not mean just a capacity for allowing the other person to speak. He must really listen so that he can gain a deep understanding of the person who seeks his help. It is only in this way that he will ever come to understand and appreciate the capacities of the individual. It is only on the basis of such an appreciation that he will be able to point in the direction of real development.

In a sense, the director should be a sort of sounding board for the other person. It is in the dialogue itself that the person will begin to develop. Dialogue, however, is not a matter of questions and answers. There must be real thought and mutual understanding and sympathy. It will frequently be most helpful for the director to avoid giving direct and immediate answers to practical problems. He may be of most use to the other person if he can ask questions which stimulate thought and personal decision. The result of this is a kind of auto-direction which develops responsibility and confidence. When to give answers and when to ask questions is not a decision that can be made as a general principle. The director must determine this by whatever is most conducive to the real growth of the individual.

As there is an increase in confidence and the assumption of responsibility, there is also a deepening of motivation. As this occurs the person is in a much better position to develop in his spiritual life. It is then that he can begin to make practical decisions on really solid grounds. As he learns to do this he becomes far more capable of drawing out his spirituality from his own life, personality and abilities. He should be in process of reaching the point at which decisions are his own, even though they may have been formulated as the result of dialogue with the director. The fact of his Christian transformation is being brought gradually to the level of reflexive consciousness.

The director also has, of course, the responsibility to teach the person certain elements of the spiritual life which are essential but which may not evolve spontaneously. Such would be spiritual practices as meditation and particular examen. This can be done in a very non-technical manner. If we simply take these two practices as an example I can explain what I mean. I would not think that the best way to introduce a person to meditation would be to give him a book and send him off on his own. Methods of meditation may vary and it may take some time to find a method which is of the greatest value to the individual. He should begin with short periods which are extended both spontaneously and by intent. What is most important, however, is that he be aware of what he is doing and what it is supposed to accomplish. Sometimes we make the mistake of thinking that the effect of the meditation should be the formulation of some resolution which carries over into the day. While this may be both profitable and useful, it is not the end result desired. Frequently such a resolution is forgotten or broken in a matter of moments, and the meditation is still useful. Its real success can be determined only over a period of time. Such success can best be determined by answering a question some time after the effort of meditation has begun: Has this daily effort at formal prayer had the result of making prayer more spontaneous in the whole life of the individual? Is he more conscious of the presence of God within him? If he can answer this affirmatively, then the meditation has had its effect. This is true no matter what distractions or lack of resolution may have seemed to be involved in the prayer of any given day. Particular examen works in the same way. It is nothing more than the effort to be conscious of one's faults and to ask God's help in overcoming them. Again, some of its results are long-range.

What results are finally to be hoped for from spiritual direction? It might be well to stress that the direction in itself is not what produces the results. At least, it does not produce results as though these came merely from the human effort alone. It is the inter-relationship of persons elevated to a transformed Christian state, and so it is in reality the action of God which produces the results, although the human causality is present. The summary of the results is sanctity. It is expressed at conscious level in the awareness of one's relationship to God and neighbor. It is a fullness of Christian life and a form of mystical prayer.

CHAPTER THIRTEEN:

PRAYER AND MYSTICISM

IN THE PRECEDING pages I have attempted to present the Christian experience within the framework of sacramental structures. The reason for this is that in the sacraments we have a sort of summary of the Christian life. The sacraments seem to touch us at all the critical moments of our earthly existence. It is through them that we are born into the divine life and through them that this life is nourished. But the sacraments are given moments in a continuous existence, even though their influence in our lives is more than momentary.

The sacraments, however, are not magic. If they are to have their effects, then we must be conscious of those effects. They demand our response. The form of that response is both active and prayerful. We respond by means of our love of God and neighbor, but we give meaning to that activity by means of continued growth in the life of prayer. Without real prayer the sacraments will begin to lose their meaning. Furthermore, as that response of prayer grows, it begins to become a form of mystic prayer, and it is this mystical response that I think is an absolute necessity.

For the true Christian, mysticism is a necessity and not a luxury. Unfortunately the term "mysticism" is frequently misunderstood. It is taken to refer to a variety of extraordinary manifestations, such as visions, etc. When I speak here of mysticism I do not mean that every Christian should himself experience the visions, ecstasies and transports of joy that are described by many of the well known mystical writers. Even the greatest of the mystics considered these things as extraordinary and they were quite careful to emphasize that they were by no means essential to the life of real prayer which is mysticism. Therefore, when I speak of mysticism as a necessity for the Christian what I am speaking of is a growing consciousness of one's living union in the life of the Trinity. It should also be stated that this consciousness is not something that is simply self-induced. It is a gift and it can be given in a variety of ways, or, at least, it can manifest itself in a variety of ways. It may, for example, begin to appear in the form of that real interest in others of which I spoke in earlier chapters. In other words, it can manifest itself quite visibly in the form of a real love of neighbor. It could, therefore, exist even in the person who is not conscious of any more than vocal prayer in himself.

Let me describe briefly what I mean when I speak of mysticism in the life of the Christian. The Christian lives in union with God. This union is always present, even when the individual does not think of it. His mind may be occupied with a thousand and one things which occur in his daily life, and yet in all of these God is present. But if there are real efforts at prayer, then gradually there is an increased consciousness of the presence of God within us. Prayer should change us, not change God.

Prayer is frequently prayer of petition. In our need and desire for change and improvement we turn to God for help. But keep in mind what prayer is supposed to do. As children we learned to ask for God's help, but it was usually help in childish things. We looked for success in games and examinations. We prayed that rain would not disturb our picnics, that the abundance of candy would never fail, that our parents would allow us to do whatever it was that we wanted to do at the moment. When all of these things didn't happen it was a bit of a shock to us, but (perhaps rather stoically) we tried again. It is only as we grow up that we realize what a prayer of petition really is. Not every prayer demands a miracle, because the things that we pray for are usually not worth miracles. No matter how well we pray there will still be rain at some of our picnics, the candy will still run out some day, and we won't always have our own way.

The mistake that we make as children is to think that our prayer is going to change God's mind. It is as though he has not yet decided what to do and we offer our help in his decision-making process, or as though he has made up his mind and we hope to set him straight about things. Prayer is too often an effort to change God's will. It is a very anthropomorphic vision of God, a vision that is limited by the limitations of our own temporality. He becomes the workman and we become the overseers. What we must keep in mind is that the real purpose of prayer is to change us and to bring our wills into line with God's will. Our prayer should be ultimately a prayer for union with God and with each other.

There is no possible way in which I can do justice to the notion of prayer in a few pages. All I can do is to present some ideas on it. I will present these ideas in the form of a descriptive narrative. It will then be up to each reader to use his own experience in order to supplement what I have to say.

When you first begin to pray your prayer is vocal. You learn prayers as a child and you repeat them by memory. Gradually you progress beyond this stage to the point at which you use your own words. For the most part this prayer will usually be prayer of petition. It will center on your needs. You move on to the beginnings of mental prayer, but here it is almost vocal, although you may no longer form the words with your mouth, but only in your mind. At this stage too it will often be prayer of petition. You will, however, begin to realize that now your needs are not simply things that it would be nice to have. You begin to look at yourself and you realize that there is much that must be changed. You begin to ask God for help in a transformation that you finally realize is necessary. You find that this transformation is actually beginning to occur. Now prayer of thanksgiving becomes more important. But you know too that while you have much for which to be thankful, you are a rather unprofitable servant. You begin to turn to prayer of contrition. Gradually all of your prayers begin to become united in a prayer of adoration. You begin to realize that God is really working within you, and you adore him. Words become less necessary. Discursive prayer begins to turn to contemplation of the goodness which is God. You may arrive at the point where you cannot speak in prayer at all. You simply look at God in wonder. You can do no more than speak his name.

Your prayer becomes just the one word, "God!" And even then you realize that even this one word is too much. God is beyond your words and yet he is within you. All the words in the world are not sufficient to contain him, and one word is too much to express his simplicity and perfection.

At no stage of this prayer will you withdraw from your daily occupations, but now the thousand and one things that you were always doing become different. They have a new meaning. All of them can be done in union with God. Even this awareness begins to change. You start to realize that you do not contain God. He contains you. He has taken you into his own life. His life has become yours. His love has become yours. His knowledge has become yours. And this leads you to the knowledge that love of God and love of neighbor are inseparable. You begin to treat your neighbor as you know that God treats him and as you know that God treats you. And you now know that in this whole process it was never really you who were accomplishing all that happened. It was always God, even at those times when you did not realize his presence.

All of this manifests itself in your life and activity. You begin to take everything as it should be taken. You know what is important and what is unimportant. What is important is no longer the wonderful things that you may once have dreamed of doing. The important thing is now to do all the small things that make up your earthly life. You live only to please God in all that you do. Your idea of the meaning of martyrdom changes. The martyr is one who bears witness to God by giving his life. But you now realize that giving your life does not mean waiting in idleness for the chance to give its last moment. You must give every moment. It is a waste of time to spend our lives waiting for the chance to do something big. It might very well happen that the moment will come when I have to face God, and only then will I realize that I was never given anything to do except the small things and I have left them all undone.

CHAPTER FOURTEEN:

THE INTERIOR LIFE

I HAVE NOW spoken of the sacraments and of the prayer of the Christian. In the course of some of the chapters I had made considerable use of the writings of Saint Paul. In order to do this I found it necessary to rearrange the order of many of Paul's statements, since he was writing letters and was not writing an orderly account of the spiritual progress of the life of the Christian. In the present chapter I would like to consider one of the books of Saint Teresa of Avila. In her *Interior Castle* she makes a conscious effort to be orderly in her presentation, and, for the most part, she is quite successful. She writes from the viewpoint of the true mystic, and she writes in such a way that the ordinary reader can readily identify himself with the kind of experience of spiritual growth of which she speaks. However, if we are to arrive at the reality with which she is concerned, we may find one thing which must be overcome. This is the slight obstacle of a figurative language which may at times seem outdated. She does not write as a scientific theologian with a more or less fixed terminology. She is writing from her own experience and consciously uses a great deal of symbolism in order to express her thoughts. Here we shall have to try to pass through this symbolism to the reality which lies underneath. It might, perhaps, be correct to say that we must transfer her symbolism into a symbolism of our own so that we can see the identity of experience in both instances.

Saint Teresa presents the spiritual life by describing the soul as composed of seven mansions, arranged in concentric spheres, in the center of which is God himself. This description is in itself significant. Once this has been set as the basic symbolism of her description, spiritual progress can no longer be accomplished by a series of external stages, but by a series of "interiorizations" which seem at first to be withdrawal from the world, and then, by the time one reaches the prayer of union, are recognizable as transformative union with God. This union not only transforms the individual who undergoes it, but also transforms the world, since the union itself is directed to love of neighbor (and, in fact, this becomes its validating principle).

Teresa begins with her analogy of the soul as a series of mansions. "I begin to think of the soul as if it were a castle made of a single diamond or of very clear crystal, in which there are many rooms, just as in heaven there are many mansions."[1] The first of these mansions is the beginning of spiritual progress. Here the soul is in a state of grace, but is still surrounded by temptation. It receives illumination from the central mansion, but this illumination still remains obscured (not so much because of a lack in the light as because of the lack of receptivity of the individual).[2]

In the second mansions the soul is involved in activity, most of which centers about the practice of prayer and the acquiring of virtues. "This chapter has to do with those who have already begun to practice prayer and who realize the importance of not remaining in the first Mansions, but who often are not yet resolute enough to leave those Mansions, and will not avoid occasions of sin, which is a very perilous condition."[3] In this stage the soul advances by means of conversations, sermons, books, sicknesses and trials. There are hindrances and imperfections, and at this stage one should not seek consolations. The individual must now labor diligently to bring his will into conformity with the will of God.

At the stage of the third mansions the soul has already attained a high degree of virtue, but it must realize that there is still need for further perfection. "I believe that through His goodness there are many such souls in the world; they are most desirous not to offend His Majesty; they avoid committing even venial sins; they love doing penance; they spend hours in recollection; they use their time well; they practice works of charity toward their neighbors; and they are very careful in their speech and dress and in the government of their household if they have one."⁴ At this stage of development it becomes necessary to emphasize the need of complete love of God and complete giving of oneself to Him. "Without complete self-renunciation, the state is very arduous and oppressive, because, as we go along, we are laboring under the burden of our miserable nature, which is like a great load of earth and has not to be borne by those who reach the later Mansions."⁵ Here it becomes necessary to place oneself under the guidance of a good director, so that it becomes possible to practice obedience. The director should be a man who is detached and who may enable the person to know himself.

It is in the fourth mansions that we first come to what Saint Teresa calls supernatural prayer. By this she seems to mean that here human effort is of no avail. This effort may take one as far as the third mansions, but at this point God takes over and draws the progress along as he wills (although she makes it quite clear that she is aware that divine activity is involved in the whole process). It is also here that she makes a distinction between "spiritual sweetnesses" (*contentos*) and "spiritual consolations" (*gustos*). The difference between the two is in their source. The sweetnesses can be induced by human activity and amount to feelings of satisfaction at prayer and relationship with God. Teresa likens these to the noisy entrance of water through conduits into a basin. Consolations, on the other hand, can have their source only in God, and seem to well up from within the soul, so that they arise quietly and without our activity. These consolations are what she also calls the prayer of quiet. While it comes from within, it is not humanly produced but comes from the indwelling of God. In her description of this she is quite reminiscent of Meister Eckhart. "I do not think that this happiness has its source in the heart at all. It arises in a much more interior part, like something of which the springs are very deep; I think this must be the centre of the soul, as I have already realized and as I will explain hereafter."⁶ At this stage the soul is well advised to allow God to take over. "As I understand it, the soul whom the Lord has been pleased to lead into this mansion will do best to act as I have said. Let it try, without forcing itself or causing any turmoil, to put a stop to all discursive reasoning, yet not to suspend the understanding, nor to cease from all thought, though it is well for it to remember that it is in God's presence and Who this God is. If feeling this should lead it into a state of absorption, well and good; but it should not try to understand what this state is, because that is a gift bestowed upon the will. The will, then, should be left to enjoy it, and should not labor except for uttering a few loving words, for although in such a case one may not be striving to cease from thought, such cessation often comes, though for a very short time."[7]

In the fifth mansions we find the prayer of union, at least in its incipient stages (also referred to as Spiritual Betrothal). This is a very high form of prayer life, and yet Teresa says that there are really very few who do not enter these mansions. It is a state to be desired, but one cannot acquire it for himself. It must be given to him by God.

One of the problems that Saint Teresa mentions is that of certitude. How can one be certain that what he experiences is really this prayer of quiet? Her answer is quite unusual (at least, at first glance), because when looked at from the viewpoint of human evidence, the only evidence is really a kind of instinct. She says: "God implants Himself in the interior of that soul in such a way that, when it returns to itself, it cannot possibly doubt that God has been in it and it has been in God; so firmly does this truth remain within it that, although for years God may never grant it that favour again, it can neither forget it nor doubt that it has received it (and this quite apart from the effects which remain within it, and of which I will speak later)."[8]

It is in her discussion of the fifth mansions that Teresa uses the famous image of the silkworm. The silkworm (soul) takes life through heat (Spirit). It spins its silk and builds the house (Christ) in which it will die. When, finally, it is dead to the world it comes from its cocoon, a butterfly, and takes flight. The things that delighted it as a worm are no longer of interest, and it flies, where before it had only been able to crawl.

It is also here that she begins to speak of love of neighbor. "But here the Lord asks only two things of us: love for His Majesty and love for our neighbor. . . . The surest sign that we are keeping these two commandments is, I think, that we should really be loving our neighbor, for we cannot be sure if we are loving God, although we may have good reasons for believing that we are, but we can know quite well if we are loving our neighbor."[9]

Within the stage of these fifth mansions there begins Spiritual Betrothal. Here Teresa describes it in terms of its inception. * "It seems to me that this union has not yet reached the point of spiritual betrothal, but is rather like what happens in our earthly life when two people are about to be betrothed. . . [At this stage the lovers meet in order to determine whether they are suited for each other]. . . . We can compare this kind of union to a short meeting of that nature because it is over in the very shortest time. All giving and taking have now come to an end and in a secret way the soul sees who this Spouse is that she is to take."[10]

The stage of the sixth mansions is the real point of the Spiritual Betrothal. This stage is actually quite peculiar. In it there is a combination of pleasure and pain which presents an enigma not only to the understanding of the stage, but also an enigma within the very person of the one who undergoes the experience. The soul has arrived at a union with God which may manifest itself in visions, both imaginary and intellectual. It is in the final stage of preparation for Spiritual Marriage, and yet it is afflicted both from within and without. It is faced with its own bodily weakness, by reason of which it may even become ill. The person finds himself misunderstood and persecuted. In fact, he may even suffer more at times from being accepted than from his rejection. He feels his rejection as a rejection of God, since it is God who is

---

*It might be well to note here that Saint Teresa's analogy is based on the marriage customs of her time. Young men and women were segregated and the marriage was arranged by the two families. Before the actual betrothal the couple were introduced to each other, but only briefly and in the presence of a chaperone.

the source of what he undergoes. At the same time he fears acceptance, because the acceptance may be directed to him more than to God, and he realizes his own unworthiness and wants all the praise to be directed to God. He can also suffer at the hands of those to whom he goes for direction. He may be misunderstood and told what he has experienced is false, and this causes affliction by creating doubts (a source of even greater suffering, because although he would like to accept the decision of his confessor, he is so convinced of the truth of what he has experienced, that he knows the confessor to be wrong).

From within there come sufferings which may, I think, be categorized into two general areas. The first of these is the acute awareness of one's own unworthiness. The individual is well aware of his own sinfulness and is afflicted by the awareness that all the sin he has committed has been committed "within God" (which is to say that he now realizes that his whole existence is inseparable from that of God). Secondly, there is the suffering which is created by the person's desire to leave earth and enter into complete union with God.

The seventh mansions constitute the final stage, that of Spiritual Marriage. The soul has now reached its innermost mansion. It has found that it has God in its own center. It now becomes fully united to God. This is even more intense a union than was present in the prayer of union. The best explanation of this new union, for Saint Teresa, "is as if the ends of two wax candles were joined so that the light they give is one: the wicks and the wax and the light are all one; yet afterwards the one candle can be perfectly well separated from the other and the candles become two again, or the wick may be withdrawn from the wax. But here it is like rain falling from the heavens into a river or a spring; there is nothing but water there and it is impossible to divide or separate the water belonging to the river from that which fell from the heavens."[11] However, in this last stage of spiritual development there is another change which is, in a sense, even more amazing. Teresa says that in the earlier stages the soul has been given to raptures which cause it to lose contact with the senses. In this highest stage of all these raptures do not occur, or at least there is no external sign that they are occurring. The soul remains in full possession of its faculties and the person is quite capable of performing his duties. The only difference between this and the first stage of prayer (and it is indeed an essential difference) is that while in both cases the soul is capable of performing its duties, the motive and mode have changed entirely. While in its first stages the soul was a bit self-centered and was conscious of its own part, in this stage the soul is constantly directed to God and neighbor, and is aware that its own part is worthless. Connected with this difference is the fact that earlier the soul had not desired death because it feared it. Now it does not desire death because it wants to serve God and bring others to him.

These few pages are a rather sketchy outline of the *Interior Castle,* but I hope that it is at least sufficient for our purposes here. I want to use it to show that the reality of which Teresa is speaking is the same as that reality of which Paul spoke, and which the Christian must experience in his own life. Paul had presented the spiritual life in terms of Christian transformation. He had made it quite clear that the activity of the Christian is founded in this transformation. In the next few pages I will attempt to demonstrate that Teresa is saying at least this. There is also the fact that the human mind has the greatest difficulty in reconciling the coexistence of the finite and the infinite. This difficulty manifests itself in our tendency either to attempt to make ourselves infinite or to reduce God to our finitude. In doing this we either distort ourselves or attempt to distort God (which again results in the distortion of ourselves). In the process of spiritual development this difficulty also arises. There it manifests itself in the form of self-sufficiency (as though we were infinite) and our actions are mistakenly taken as the cause of our own self development; or we may distort God's action by considering that it is so immersed in ours that we have no need for any human effort to transcend our own finitude (in this case we can fall into a kind of quietism).

Let us again consider the *Interior Castle* and concentrate on those statements which are most significant. The first point is in her reference to the difference between thought (imagination) and intellect.[12] She had become concerned at the fact that even when she seemed to be occupied with God, her thought still continued to be confused and excited. At this stage she answers the problem by pointing to the difference that she had learned between imagination and intellect. While the former continues to wander, the latter can remain focused on God. It seems to me that this solution can be taken a bit further. What really seems to be happening is that at this stage (the fourth mansions) the soul is on the verge of prayer of union. This is the beginning of what she calls supernatural prayer. I would say that at this point there was a change in her consciousness of God's activity. The person who proceeds this far in the life of prayer has by now become aware that actions which seemed to be his own at earlier stages were actually the working of God.

Thus at this stage the individual is beginning to experience and enter into the simplicity of God. However, humanity, with its fragmentation of being and activity, stands in the way and the soul finds this frustrating until it realizes what is happening. Thus instead of speaking merely in terms of imagination and intellect, it might be better here to speak of the first experiential knowledge of the internal coexistence of the human and the divine in the Christian. Humanity seems to stand in the way of entrance into simplicity. It is only in higher stages that this coexistence can be reconciled experientially.

Again, when she speaks of sweetnesses and consolations, there is the apparent presence of this same kind of tension.[13] The sweetness comes in from outside and noisily (i.e., with human activity). The consolations well up from within and silently. This would seem again to be a differing awareness of divine activity. It would seem that at this stage (prayer of quiet) there is an experience of divine causality which is directly conscious but is only incipient at the reflexive level. It should be noted, however, that Teresa insists that the consolations are not necessary and should not be sought.[14] We might then say that while union with God is necessary for salvation, our consciousness of that union need not reach the stage that we associate with *extraordinary* mystic experience.

It is also in these fourth mansions that discursive reasoning becomes less of a necessity. The awareness of God's presence seems to become more intuitive. What had earlier depended upon the activity of human understanding now seems to become the object of the human will in union with the divine will. This was the meaning of the text quoted earlier in reference to the cessation of discursive reasoning at this stage.[15]

It is in the fifth mansions that one finally comes to the direct realization that heaven on earth is within ourselves.[16] This union with God is expansive, in the sense that the truth of his presence is proven by the giving of one's self to neighbor. Yet, while this may be a test of the validity of the union, it is not a proof. There is, in fact, no proof which is external to the union itself. The soul is convinced of its union by the very presence of God. "God implants Himself in the interior of that soul in such a way that, when it returns to itself, it cannot possibly doubt that God has been in it and it has been in God; so firmly does this truth remain within it that, although for years God may never grant it that favour again, it can neither forget it nor doubt that it has received it (and this quite apart from the effects which remain within it, and of which I will speak later). This certainty of the soul is very material. But now you will say to me: How did the soul see it and understand it if it can neither see nor understand? I am not saying that it saw it at the time, but that it sees it clearly afterwards, and not because it is a vision, but because of a certainty which remains in the soul, which can be put there only by God."[17]

This union is not merely a union of grace. I would think that when Teresa speaks of this she is really saying that God's presence is far more than merely the presence of a gift within us. I mean that it is not simply a case of God's granting us some gift external to himself. He is himself present in such a way that his own life is lived in us. It is a presence which cannot be doubted, but also cannot be adequately explained in any human fashion. Teresa wrote on one occasion: "Once I was recollected with companionship that I always have in my soul, when I felt that God was within my soul in such a way that I recalled the occasion on which Saint Peter said: 'Thou art the Christ, the Son of the living God.' For even so was the living God within my soul. This is not like other visions, for it reinforces faith, so that it is impossible to doubt that the Trinity is, by presence, power and essence, within our souls. It is of the very greatest benefit to understand this truth. I was astounded to see such majesty in anything as lowly as my soul. Then I heard these words: 'It is not lowly, daughter, for it is made in My image.' I also learned several things about the reason why God delights more in souls than in other things He has created; these things were so subtle that, though the understanding comprehended them quickly, I cannot explain them."[18]

It is within the fifth mansions also that there is another change in awareness. Whereas before Teresa had tended to speak of the life of God within us, she now begins to reverse this position and to speak of the life of man within God. In conjunction with this she seems to see even more clearly the unchangeableness of God and the fact that it is we who change. She says: "When I say He will be our Mansion, and we can construct it for ourselves and hide ourselves in it, I seem to be suggesting that we can subtract from God or add to Him. But of course we cannot possibly do that! We can neither subtract from, nor add to, God, but we can subtract from, and add to, ourselves, just as these little silkworms do."[19] This transfer of awareness creates the beginnings of a real tension between the incarnational and the eschatological aspects of the spiritual life. The soul is now aware of God's presence even in this life, and this has begun to transfer itself into the awareness of the presence of the soul within God. It is the real beginning of death of self in the presence of God; so that one is in a quandary as to whether he should be making the choice of life in God here and now, or life in God in death. "The silkworm has of necessity to die; and it is this which will cost you the most; for death comes more easily when one can see oneself living a new life, whereas our duty now is to continue living this present life, and yet to die of our own free will."[20] This conflict is only solved in a workable manner in the later stages, as we shall see.

The same tension is furthered (and it is in the furthering that it will find its resolution) by an awareness of one's responsibility to love of neighbor. Teresa writes: "Here the Lord asks only two things of us: love for His Majesty and love for our neighbor. . . The surest sign that we are keeping these two commandments is, I think, that we should really be loving our neighbor; for we cannot be sure if we are loving God, although we may have good reasons for believing that we are, but we can know quite well if we are loving our neighbor."[21] Prayer and union with God should not draw us back into ourselves, for this would be selfishness. Instead, it should open us to an active love of neighbor. "When I see people very diligently trying to discover what kind of prayer they are experiencing and so completely wrapt up in their prayers that they seem afraid to stir, or to indulge in a moment's thought, lest they should lose the slightest degree of the tenderness and devotion which they have been feeling, I realize how little they understand of the road to the attainment of union. They think that the whole thing consists in this. But no, sisters, no; what the Lord desires is works. If you see a sick woman to whom you can give some help, never be affected by the fear that your devotion will suffer, but take pity on her; if she is in pain, you should feel pain too; if necessary, fast so that she may have your food, not so much for her sake as because you know it to be your Lord's will."[22]

The experiential tension is intensified in the sixth mansions. There is a strange mixture of agony and pleasure. This is not a mixture in the sense that the soul fluctuates between the two. Rather, the agony is itself the pleasure. It is a tension between the fact of an already existing union with God and a desire for the completion of that union. "Although no sound is heard, the soul is very well aware that it has been called by God, so much so that sometimes, especially at first, it begins to tremble and complain, though it feels nothing that causes it affliction. It is conscious of having been most delectably wounded, but cannot say how or by whom; but it is certain that this is a precious experience and it would be glad if it were never to be healed of that wound... Although occasionally the experience lasts for a certain length of time, it goes and comes again; it is, in short, never permanent, and for that reason it never completely enkindles the soul; for, just as the soul is about to become enkindled, the spark dies, and leaves the soul yearning once again to suffer that loving pain of which it is the cause... It is perfectly clear that it is a movement of which the source is the Lord, Who is unchangeable; and its effects are not like those of other devotions whose genuineness we doubt because of the intense absorption of the joy which we experience. Here all the senses and faculties are active, and there is no absorption... It may be that you wonder why greater security can be felt about this than about other things. For the following reasons, I think. First, because so delectable a pain can never be bestowed upon the soul by the devil... Secondly, this delectable tempest comes from another region than those over which he has authority. Thirdly, great advantages accrue to the soul, which, as a general rule, becomes filled with a determination to suffer for God's sake and to desire to have many trials to endure, and to be very much more resolute in withdrawing from the pleasures and intercourse of this world, and other things like them."[23]

One should realize that we are here speaking of interpersonal relationships and not merely of abstract principles (even though our language will at times be somewhat deceptive). At this point human effort appears insignificant and is seen in such union with the divine activity that it pales before it.[24]

It is in the seventh mansions that the conflicts are resolved at an experiential level. The union of human and divine is felt not only in the center of the soul, but extends itself even to activity. This is indicated in Saint Teresa's example of the two candles and the mingling of the water.[25] The union is so thorough that there is a total forgetfulness of self.[26] Tensions are resolved and the soul is now even more anxious to continue to live in this life.

Union has already been attained and there is a most vivid desire to extend this union to others.[27] The forgetfulness of self is not now manifested in raptures which withdraw one from his surroundings. Human activity is carried on in a normal manner, but there is a continuing consciousness of its union with God's own activity. There is, then, a consciousness of the unity of the divine and human causality.[28]

There is finally the conscious awareness, already indicated at earlier stages, that God has not entered into us. Somehow we have entered into God. The soul has an awareness that the Three Persons are one, and it has become one with them. The knowledge and love of the saint for God are the knowledge and love of God for himself, and this knowledge and love are so personal that they are the divine persons of the Son and the Spirit. "I have had with me this presence of the Three Persons, of which I spoke earlier, until today, which is that of the Commemoration of Saint Paul. They have been continually present in my soul; and, as I was accustomed to have only Jesus Christ with me, I had supposed all the time that the presence of the Three Persons was to some extent a hindrance to this; the Lord told me I was wrong to think of things of the soul in the same terms as of those of the body: I must realize that the two are very different and that the soul has a capacity for great fruition. This seemed to be shown me by the illustration of a sponge which takes up and absorbs water; just so my soul was filled with the Godhead and in a certain sense it had within itself the fruition and the possession of the Three Persons. I also heard these words: *'Labor not to hold Me enclosed within thyself but to enclose thyself within Me.'* It seemed that these Three Persons were present within my soul and that I saw Them there, and they communicated Themselves to all created things, and never either failed to do this or ceased to be with me."[29]

The correlation of divine and human causality has reached its most elevated conscious awareness. The finite cannot contain the Infinite, and if it tries to do so it will distort itself. The Infinite can contain the finite and in doing so transforms it without distorting it. Sin becomes unthinkable, because the soul would now have to sin while realizing that it has its very being in God. Sin would be suicidal. "Let us imagine that God is like a very large and beautiful mansion or palace. The palace, then, as I say, is God Himself. Now can the sinner go away from it in order to commit his misdeeds? Certainly not; these abominations and dishonorable actions and evil deeds which we sinners commit are done within the palace—that is, within God."[30] Mary and Martha, the contemplative and the practical, have become united in one so as now to be inseparable. Contemplation and works are inseparable. The soul is one with God and desires nothing but his will. It gives itself totally to him by giving itself totally to others, regardless of the cost to self.

Thus, in spite of differences in descriptions, images and language, Paul and Teresa arrive at a realization of the same reality. This is quite explicit if we compare Teresa's statements to what Paul says in the Epistle to the Philippians: "For as I see it, living means Christ and dying something even better. But if living on here means having my labor bear fruit, I cannot tell which to choose. I am undecided between the two, for I long to depart and be with Christ, for that is far, far better, and yet your needs make it very necessary for me to stay on here. I am convinced of this, and so I know that I shall stay on and serve you all, to help you to develop and to be glad in your faith. So you will find in me fresh cause for Christian exultation, through having me with you again."[31] It is to this same awareness that our spiritual growth must tend. And it is also to this awareness that we must draw others. There is no greater service we can perform for them.

1. Saint Teresa, *Interior Castle,* in E. Allison Peers (ed.), *The Complete Works of Saint Teresa of Jesus,* London and New York, 1957[5], Vol. III, p. 201.
2. *Ibid.,* p. 210.
3. *Ibid.,* p. 227.
4. *Ibid.,* p. 221.
5. *Ibid.,* p. 227.

6. *Ibid.*, p. 237.
7. *Ibid.*, p. 243. Cf. Similar notions in *The Cloud of Unknowing*.
8. *Ibid.*, p. 251.
9. *Ibid.*, p. 261.
10. *Ibid.*, pp. 264-265.
11. *Ibid.*, p. 335.
12. *Ibid.*, p. 233.
13. *Ibid.*, pp. 236-237.
14. *Ibid.*, p. 239.
15. Cf. above, n. 7 (quoted on p. 127).
16. Cf. *ibid.*, pp. 247-248.
17. *Ibid.*, p. 251.
18. *Relations, LIV* (Peers, *op. cit.*, Vol I, p. 361).
19. *Interior Castle, loc. cit.*, p. 254.
20. *Ibid.*, p. 260.
21. *Ibid.*, p. 261.
22. *Ibid.*, pp. 262-263.
23. *Ibid.*, pp. 276-278.
24. *Ibid.*, p. 294.
25. *Ibid.*, p. 335.
26. *Ibid.*, p. 339.
27. *Ibid.*, p. 340.
28. *Ibid.*, p. 342.
29. *Relations, XVIII* (Peers, *op. cit.*, Vol. I, p. 343; italics mine).
30. *Interior Castle, loc. cit.*, p. 322.
31. Phil 1,21-26.

CHAPTER FIFTEEN

THE BLESSED VIRGIN

IN PRECEDING CHAPTERS I have spoken of growth into Christian perfection and have attempted to do so within the framework of the experience of the Christian life—an experience involving sacraments, prayer and one's state in life. In the chapter on the interior life we saw the example of the experience of one Christian, St. Teresa of Avila, who, in what she writes, shows us something of the identity of our own experience with hers.

In this chapter I propose to speak of Mary, but I also wish to present this chapter in terms of experience. The experience to which I refer is two-fold. There is, on the one hand, the experience of the Christian community as expressed in its tradition. This is the tradition that has resulted in devotion to Mary and in a theology of the place of Mary in Christian life. There is, on the other hand, the experience of Mary herself, in so far as she is the Mother of God and in so far as she is herself a Christian.

The Old Testament is in many ways a document of hope. It is a record of man's sinfulness, beginning just after his creation. But it is also a record of God's merciful promise of redemption and man's hope in that promise. The People of God live in expectation. Their hopes rise as they progress to their own land and their own king. And just when their hopes seem most likely of realization, the kingdom is broken, never to be restored. But the catastrophe is not without meaning. The prophets, God's interpreters, have already delivered the warning that the hope had been placed in the wrong things. God's promise was not to be fulfilled in the formalism of the Law, nor in the glory of an earthly kingdom, nor in the simple claim of being his people. It would only be fulfilled in his time and in his way. And the prophets express their hopes. God has promised to save, and so they await a savior. Perhaps he will be the next king.[1] Perhaps one of the high priests.[2] Perhaps a great prophet.[3] Perhaps some great servant of God.[4] All hopes, but none of them certainties, for, while God has committed himself to his people, the completion of that commitment remains shrouded in mystery.

But God does fulfill his promise, and the fulfillment begins with a young girl. She too lives in the same hope and the same uncertainty of the way in which it is to be fulfilled. And, perhaps without even realizing that this was the beginning of fulfillment, she says, "Yes," to the message of the angel. Through her full giving of herself to the love of God, the fulfillment of the promise begins.

With her, "Yes," God's commitment is completed, but so is the commitment of man. It is as though the whole Old Testament hope has led up to this point. There is an irrevocable commitment on both sides. In her God's presence in the world assumes a dimension that the Old Testament had never dared to hope for. God himself, through her, would become one of us.

In this commitment of Mary to God, there is one basic element that we must not lose sight of. It is the fact that we are speaking of a real, human person. Too often, I think, we tend to idealize. We think of Mary as a kind of plaster statue, highly decorated, unchangeable, untouchable, far removed from us, a majesty to be venerated. Perhaps we forget that her commitment to God was not a word spoken by a saint far removed from this life. It was spoken by a young girl who loved God, but who lived a very ordinary and poor life. It was the commitment of a real person capable of making real choices. And her free choice played its role in God's plan. Her response is not the formalism of a mere obedience to law, but the free choice of a human person in response to the freely given love of God. For to say that Mary is without sin is not at all to say that she is without choice. Free will does not mean the option of either good or evil. Real free will, used as it was meant to be, means the capacity always to choose the good without any fear that we can ever really be forced to choose what is evil. And so Mary uses her sinless freedom to accept God totally into the world.

It is the choice, this commitment, that seems to strike some of the early Fathers of the Church as the foundation for their understanding of Mary. Justin, for example, writes:

> For Eve, while still a virgin. . ., when the word of the serpent was conceived, brought forth disobedience and death. While the Virgin Mary, . . .to the angel Gabriel, who announced his joyous message, . . . answered: Be it done unto me according to thy word.[5]

Irenaeus says:

> Just as [Eve], who had a husband, Adam, while still a virgin. . .became disobedient and became the cause of death for herself and the whole human race: so also Mary, who had a husband already chosen, and while still a virgin, by her obedience became the cause of salvation for herself and the whole human race.[6]

Both of these writers draw the same basic parallel. Eve made her choice and disobeyed, thus bringing death upon all her children. Mary made her choice and obeyed, thus bringing life for all her children. Just as Eve's sin was the sin of all humanity, so in some sense Mary's, "Yes," was the acceptance of all humanity. For it was this act of loving obedience which made Christ present in the world, and so changed the meaning of history from beginning to end. It was also the, "Yes," of the Church which, like Mary, must bring Christ into the world. We, as members of that Church, are begotten through her obedience. Augustine writes:

> That one woman is both mother and virgin, not only in spirit but even bodily. She is mother in spirit, not of our head, who is the Savior himself, from whom she is spiritually born (since all who believe in him, among whom she is included, are called *children of the bridegroom* [Mt 9,15]), but certainly she is mother of the members, which means ourselves, because she cooperated in love in order for the faithful, who are the members of the Head, to be born in the Church; but bodily she is mother of the Head himself.[7]

Therefore, the parallel that is being drawn also involves a parallel between Mary and the Church, a parallel which was also seen by the Second Vatican Council.[8]

Yet we must avoid the idea that this concept of Mary's obedience is a passive thing. It is not. Obedience is not mere acquiescence, it is active participation. It is freely chosen commitment. In the parallels that are drawn by the Fathers quoted above, Mary is not treated merely as a passive element in a foreordained plan, but as a person choosing to play her part in that plan. Her importance lies not merely in the fact that something happened to her, but in the fact that she chose to do something. She became the gateway to God's presence in the world in Christ because she chose to obey.

In the tradition of the Church, devotion to Mary has for centuries held a very prominent place. When Vatican II spoke of this tradition it praised it and said that it should continue.[9] But it also spoke of excess and of narrowness. It is possible to make the position of Mary into something that it should not be, if we begin to speak of her in terms that make her stand alone, apart from the rest of the Church, or if we speak of her in terms that would create the impression that she is somehow outside the realm of the salvific act of her own Son. On the other hand, it is also possible to destroy her proper position by narrowing down our concepts of it to the point of seeing her merely as another Christian. It would seem to me that the proper way to view devotion to Mary and the theological position of Mary must both involve an awareness of Mary as human and as choosing, as well as an awareness of the fact that her choice was the choice to accept a freely given gift from God.

Therefore, it does not seem enough to say that Mary was the Mother of God and to rest the case there, as though all had been said that could be said. Instead, I think we must see her, as the Second Vatican Council saw her, in relation to Christ and the Church.[10] As to the way in which these two relationships are to be put together, I think a clue is given in the passage quoted above from Saint Augustine. She is mother in flesh of the Head of the Body. She is mother in spirit of the members of the Body. It was her cooperation in love which made possible the birth of the members of Christ. And yet she too is a member, spiritually born of her Son who is the firstborn of many members. Her active participation in the will of God in the conception and birth of the Son of God is the type or exemplar of all Christian participation in the begetting of Christ in the world. This begetting of Christ is the continual concern of the Church and of each of its members. This is precisely what is taking place in the conferral and reception of the sacraments, in the growth into depth of prayer and in the living of one's life in Christ.

We speak of Mary as Mother of God, as assumed into heaven, as mediating grace, as co-redeeming. Yet all of these are terms which can be understood in the framework of her relationship to Christ and the Church. The Church too is the virginal bride giving constant birth to Christ. The Church too is the immaculate bride. The Church too is the people assumed in the newness of heavenly life. The Church too is the mediator of grace, not simply in a sacramental system, but in the fact that grace exists only in the humanity of the Church and not as though it were an independent reality in itself. The Church mediates grace by its open receptivity to God, in which it receives and makes real God's grace in the world. The Church is also co-redemptive, since it continues to make present the risen and redeeming Christ for all men. Mary is, in all of these things, the pre-eminent member of the Church. Her sinlessness, her assumption, her mediation, her active co-redemption all belong to the Church since they belong to her as member of that Church. And they all belong to her and to the Church only in virtue of the redemption in Christ Jesus. They never replace that redemption; they depend totally upon it. We are, all of us, united in Christ as one. Therefore, in Mary's attainment of that summit of redemption, we also in some way reach it, even while we are still in progress toward it. It is similar to Paul's awareness of the fact that we all share in the fullness of Christ, even while we still struggle to reach that fullness.

In view of this it is much easier to see how the Church's faith in the gift given to Mary gradually attained the level of an expression of faith in terms of Immaculate Conception or Assumption into heaven. It recognized in her the already existing presence of the concrete reality of the Church's continued hope. These are not merely "doctrines" that happened to reach a point of definition. They are, instead, doctrines which express the gradually evolving recognition of the implications of a reality. That reality is the presence of the redeeming Christ in the Church, in each member of the Church, and in Mary as the most significant member of that Church.

Devotion to Mary is not merely sentimentalism, nor is it merely a pleasant reality in the life of the Church. It is, rather, the visible emergence of a real relationship between ourselves and her—a relationship that arises from our mutual life in her Son. If we lose the devotion, then we run the risk of becoming blind to the reality that gave rise to it. If we lose the awareness of the real basis for the devotion, then we run the risk of extremism. But if we see and reflect upon the reality of the common life of every Christian in Christ, then the devotion is a necessary part of Christian fullness. It is founded in a deep realization of the communion of saints and the real acceptance of the mutual concern that all Christians have for each other.

I mentioned earlier the idea of Mary as the focal point of the hopes of the Old Testament. I would add now that we can also see her as the focal point of the fulfillment of those same hopes in the New Testament. Not a focal point in addition to Christ, but only in union with Christ and leading directly to him. Her experience in the full acceptance of the will of God, in her active acceptance, is to some degree identifiable with our experience of our own acceptance of God. The Church's historical experience in terms of both theology and devotion are expressions of that same reality. Her, "Yes," is also our, "Yes," and in that acceptance of Christ we also share a mutual love and concern that goes past the limits of time and space. We share in a communion whose ultimate foundation is Christ, present in Mary, present in the whole Church, present in all humanity, present in each one of us.

1. Cf. Is 7,1-25.

2. For references to the kingly and priestly Messiahs, cf. *The Ancient Library of Qumran,* by Frank Cross, Anchor, 1961, pp. 217-230. References may be checked in *The Dead Sea Scriptures,* translated by Theodore H. Gaster, Anchor, 1956.

3. Dt 18,15 (in context); cf. *The Christology of the Old Testament,* by Oscar Cullmann, Philadelphia, 1963.

4. Cf. Is 42,1-9; 49,1-6; 50,5-11; 52,13-53,12; Dan 7.

5. Justin, *Dialogus cum Tryphone Judaeo,* 100 (RJ 141).

6. Irenaeus, *Adversus haereses,* III, 22,4 (RJ 224).

7. Augustine, *De sancta virginitate,* 6,6 (RJ 1644).

8. Second Vatican Council, "Dogmatic Constitution on the Church," (*Lumen gentium*), Chapter VIII, nn. 60-65; cf. Walter M. Abbott, SJ, *The Documents of Vatican II,* Herder and Herder, 1966, pp. 90-93.

9. Vatican II, *Lumen gentium,* nn. 66-67; cf. Abbott, *op. cit.,* pp. 94-95.

10. Vatican II, *Lumen gentium,* n. 54; cf. Abbott, *op. cit.,* pp. 86-87.

CHAPTER SIXTEEN:

FINAL REFLECTIONS

THE FINAL CHAPTER of this book is an effort to put certain factors into proper perspective. In a sense, it is an attempt to take the practical approach of the preceding chapters and give a more theoretical explanation. The fact that I would call this a more "theoretical" chapter will not, I hope, lead the reader to think that I consider it any less important than the others. Theory is essential to practice. Our human actions are fully human only when we understand what we are doing. It is theory which ties our actions together and enables us to grasp their meaning and purpose.

How can one explain the possibility of a developing spiritual life? By the fact that we are human, we are immersed in an existence that is material. How, then, can we ever go beyond the limits of that material mode of existence? Where can we find the foundation on which to establish that the spiritual life is real and not merely illusory? There is in philosophy a very basic question which is currently engaging the interest of many philosophers and theologians. This is seen in the present interest in what is called "transcendental method." The question is whether philosophy itself is even possible. But if you think about this question, you will realize that it can only be answered by means of philosophy. In other words, you have to make use of the very thing whose existence is being questioned. You can eventually reach the answer that philosophy must be possible. If it were not, then you wouldn't be able to ask such a basic philosophical question.

In some ways the same process is present when we begin to question the possibility of a real spiritual life. In his first epistle to the Corinthians Saint Paul spoke of the fact that only the spiritual man can understand the spiritual man. Only the man who has entered into relationship to God can begin to ask questions about such a relationship. Yet to speak of such a relationship to God is to make a claim that goes beyond the limits even of imagination. We are finite human beings who claim to have entered somehow into the life and activity of the Infinite. We have been transformed so as to reach into the life of the transcendent God. But in spite of our transformation we still remain finite. How can such a thing happen?

The solution I would offer to the problem is certainly not so clear and simple as to close the question. It is, perhaps, a solution which can put the question into proper perspective. One reason that I do not think the question can be closed by a single answer is that it is a question of both theory and practice. We are speaking of the spiritual life of the individual. But every individual spends his life in a constant process of development. He is always evolving. This means that no closed theory can ever totally explain him, and no closed system of practices can totally evolve him. Furthermore, the Christian becomes the place of God's revelation in the world. If, however, the Christian remains finite, then his revelation of God will be partial and will differ from one individual to another and from one period of an individual's life to another.

It is our capacity to understand and respond as persons which first opens us to God. We are capable not merely of observing, but also of understanding the meaning of reality. Our capacity to grasp the meaning of reality also opens us to the possibility of freely choosing to be what we can and ought to be. All of this evolves within us.

A child seems at first to have his attention limited to things immediately present to him.[1] As he grows he becomes capable of going beyond the world of immediate experience. He can give meaning to things and express things in words and ideas. He is no longer limited merely to what is present, but can now begin to express what is past or future or merely possible or ought to be but is not yet. He can now move into a world which is often beyond the grasp of his personal experience. There are, of course, some new problems in this development. Meaning is quite capable of expressing error as well as truth, so that as one goes beyond the level of immediate experience he can begin to feel a certain degree of insecurity. This can also be present in one's spiritual development. Both the individual and the spiritual director must be aware of this. While trying to avoid error or deception they must also be sure to see that a sense of insecurity does not bring all development to a halt.

It is only when a person enters into this world beyond experience that he becomes capable of creative meaning. He can now set a goal beyond his own experience and move in the direction of its attainment. This creativity can lead to changes in man's surroundings and even to changes in man himself. He can make himself what he will. This self-creativity has limits, of course, but they are limits which may have to be discovered.

The capacity to grasp meaning thus reduces the world of immediate experience to one small and relatively unimportant area of the totality arrived at through the mediation of meaning. Father Lonergan writes:

> Finally, besides the transformation of nature, there is man's transformation of man himself; and in this second transformation the role of meaning is not merely directive but also constitutive. I might go on to enlarge upon the constitutive functions of meaning and many profound themes might be touched upon. For it is in the field where meaning is constitutive, that man's freedom reaches its high point. There too his responsibility is greatest. There there occurs the emergence of the existential subject, finding out for himself that he has to decide for himself what he is to make of himself.[2]

It is at this point that we can perhaps best begin to understand what God's revelation of himself does to us. We are faced with the choice of what we are going to be. Our own humanity opens to us a variety of choices, but it also places upon us a variety of limitations. Our capacity to grasp meaning presents us to ourselves as responsible persons obliged to become something. Revelation opens us to a new relationship to God, presents God to us. At the same time it presents us to ourselves as the recipients of revelation. We are no longer the same mere human beings; we are now God's children. Revelation presents us to ourselves, not as we were or as we could have been, but as we are in its reception. It interprets us. It gives us meaning. It presents us with new possibilities and new limits. Revelation expands our horizons.

The concept of horizon can also assist us in our understanding of spiritual development.[3] A man who stands in one spot and looks about him will be surrounded by a certain horizon which contains all that he can see. If he moves to another place, the horizon will be different. It will also be different if some obstacle to his view is placed or removed while he remains in the same place. The same is also true of our mental and spiritual horizons. Changes both internal and external can alter our point of view, and by so doing can also change us or make us aware of the need to change ourselves.

I wrote earlier of the child who is at first concerned with his immediate surroundings and then gradually is capable of giving meaning to the past, future, possible and imperative. This is clearly a case of expanding horizons. The reception of revelation is a further expansion. In each instance meaning can act as the mediator to bring us into contact with things still beyond the range of our immediate experience. The individual is thus faced with the possibility of development. Each actual stage of development expands his horizon and opens him to the next stage. At each stage there may be future stages as yet unsuspected, just as the child who is still learning to add figures will not yet suspect that arithmetic can expand into algebra.

If we are actually to understand the possibility of movement from one horizon to another, then we must consider the various areas in which a man can choose to operate. It is quite possible that a man may so limit his vision that any expansion of his horizon becomes difficult or even impossible. One can choose to operate in different "worlds." These worlds can be arranged in the form of a triple antithesis.

The first antithesis is that of the profane and the sacred. The world of the profane contains only the visible, material realities.

The world of the sacred goes far beyond this. As one moves from the world of the profane to the world of the sacred, he begins to see through the profane to the transcendent. The second antithesis is that of common sense (practice) and theory. The man who lives only in the world of common sense is essentially a pragmatist. He relates things to himself because of their pragmatic value. That is good which works and produces tangible results. The man in the world of theory relates objects to each other (in an explanatory fashion) because of the value of truth in itself. The third antithesis is that of the exterior and the interior. The world of the exterior is concerned with knowledge of things around us, while that of the interior involves the consciousness of oneself.

A problem may arise when the individual attempts to integrate these various worlds. It is always possible that he will try to eliminate those worlds which disturb him. He will treat them as unreal. It is conceivable then that one might try to live totally in the worlds of the profane, common sense and exteriority. This would seem to be the most irrational approach to the problem. The person would constantly be confronted with worlds whose reality he denied. This would probably become the most frustrating approach as well. There are also other possibilities. He might try to effect a compromise by eliminating elements of the worlds which he thought were contradictory. He might try to move back and forth between the worlds, like the man who enters the world of the sacred only on Sunday morning, and then spends the rest of the week in the profane.

I would not want to create the impression that I think the worlds of the profane, common sense and exterior to be evil, while those of the sacred, theoretical and interior are good. This impression can be counteracted by proper integration. Such proper integration can be achieved by allowing one world to mediate the next. None of the worlds are eliminated. Nor do we compromise them or waver between them. It is, rather, fidelity to each world which mediates the next. The person who is faithful to the profane, common sense and exterior will have to see that they are not in themselves all that is. Fidelity to them will show them all to be openings to something further.

Perhaps an example will be of some assistance at this point. Suppose that a person lives in the worlds of the profane, common sense and exterior. Association with others such as husband or wife or friends will enable one to see the reality of love. One who loves, freely gives himself to others. But love is by no means totally explainable on a pragmatic basis. The person who loves will do things from which he can gain nothing for himself. He seeks the good of the other. The man who lives in the first set of worlds will not find in them an explanation of love. He may be tempted to think that the other person must have some selfish motive. But if he himself also begins to love, he will soon begin to realize that this is no true explanation. If he is truly a man of common sense, he will want an explanation, but will not find it in his present world. Yet common sense itself will force him to see that he cannot say that love does not exist. His fidelity to the first set of worlds will lead him away from a false explanation or from no explanation at all. It will begin to move him to see that there are other worlds which go beyond the limits of his present worlds. In other words, total fidelity to one set of worlds mediates the next set. New horizons are opened, without at all destroying the first horizons. He can now realize that his life does extend beyond what formerly seemed to be its limits. Good spiritual direction is one means of helping to expand horizons in this fashion.

Once we grasp this concept of horizon, we can better understand the constant process of conversion which is the spiritual development of the individual. By "conversion" I do not mean only the sort of conversion which occurs when one moves from one religion or one denomination to another. I am speaking, rather, of four basic conversions which can be categorized as: intellectual, moral, religious and Christian.

Intellectual conversion refers basically to our insight into our own understanding. At this stage we are performing a basic human act. It is the point at which one realizes that he can understand his own experience and that this understanding is valid.[4] It is a question of understanding what understanding is.[5] It is the point at which a person's rational self-consciousness takes possession of itself. It is the level at which one begins to take charge of himself as a person. He realizes his capacity to know the truth.

The second conversion is moral conversion. This occurs on the level of decision. Once a person judges that he is capable of grasping the truth, he must next ask what he is to do about this truth. The truth can make demands upon the way in which he lives. He now faces the possibility of moral conversion. His failure to respond to such a demand would now become a conscious entrance into sin.

The third conversion of horizon is religious conversion. The intellectual and moral conversions will bring one to a new stage of openness. If we realize that the truth makes demands upon us, then we have in effect submitted ourselves to something outside of ourselves. We have come to the conclusion that our actions and our relationship to persons and things around us are governed by a reality that transcends our own desires or whims. This transcendent reality must be more than an abstraction. It must be a concrete reality. To reduce it to the level of an abstraction would mean that we were allowing our lives to be ruled by something that was less than personal. In other words, we would be submitting persons to things. But if it is a transcendent and concrete reality, it can be nothing other than God. We are at this point open to God as the basis of the intelligibility of all finite being.

The fourth and final conversion is Christian conversion. Having once admitted the existence of God in religious conversion, one must now face the person of God. The obstacle will be that of evil in the world. I have already spoken of this to some extent in the chapter on pain and death. In the face of God (as the ultimate ground of intelligibility) man is also faced with the irrationality of evil. He must now make a choice. At first this choice might seem to be the option of an evil God or the denial of any final intelligibility of reality. Yet there is a way to arrive at intelligibility. This is the possibility of conversion or transformation of evil. It may be beyond the capacity of man to transform evil, and still be within the capacity of God. Christianity, in fact, offers just such a transformation. The death of Christ offers us a redemption which concludes in resurrection.

It should be pointed out that all four of these conversions might occur even in a person who did not know of Christ. He could still recognize the possibility that God could transform evil, even while he does not know how this has occurred historically. It should also be pointed out that this series of conversions is not a simple, straight line. It might be better seen as a kind of spiral. The person who reaches the fourth conversion now has a new way of understanding himself and all reality. This means that he has arrived at a new level of intellectual conversion and the pattern will repeat itself at a higher level.

We may now turn our attention to the concept of revelation. Revelation is a self-disclosure of God to man. Insofar as it is God's act, it is infinite. But insofar as it is received by man it is finite. It is an act which involves interpersonal relationship. The result of this relationship in man is faith. Faith is personal response to personal self-giving. Yet it must be something more than mere human response. It is the self-giving of a divine person, and mere human response would wallow in its own inadequacy. Faith must be a free, human response (otherwise it would not be man's), but at the same time it must be a divine response (otherwise it would not be salvific). It is here that man transcends himself and it is here that human freedom sees its highest application. Faith is the transformation of the whole man into a new order of existence.

If we look upon revelation as a real relationship with God into which man enters, then the expression of the revelation may have a number of possibilities. It is a transforming relationship, so its expression will also be transformed. If this expression is to be in human terms, it will always be inadequate and will always follow the general patterns of human expression. As in a human relationship the expression of it is always somewhat inadequate, *a fortiori* the conceptualization and verbal expression of relationship to God will be inadequate. But this inadequacy will not mean that all true expression is impossible. Rather, it will be a case of continuing expression, constantly refined, constantly in need of further refinement and essentially inexhaustible in its possibilities.

If we apply this to the presence of Jesus in the world we may draw some conclusions about the expressibility of revelation. The acceptance of the possibility of revelation and its continuing refinement of expression should lead us to expect a definite progress in this expression of revelation.

This is precisely what we find in the Old Testament. The culmination of such a revelation could well be the presence of God in the world in such a way as to express this revelation in humanity itself. This is what we find in Jesus. Now we can certainly speak of a certain intersubjectivity in the revelation itself. In Jesus this intersubjectivity assumes the form of contact of human beings with each other. He is revelation incarnate, he is both medium and message. However, in his relationship to others (e.g., to the apostles) there is an intersubjectivity that is only gradually conceptualized. The apostles come gradually to belief in the person of Jesus because of their relationship to him.

This relationship can be expressed in human language, no matter how inadequate. Thus the relationship of Jesus to the Twelve could at first be put into everyday language. Yet this relationship is not merely to the Twelve and not only while Jesus lived on earth. Therefore it was necessary that there be a lasting expression of such a relationship. This is done in the New Testament in a literary form. The gospels and Paul's letters, for example, are an effort at a planned and permanent expression of the reality of the relationship between Jesus and the Christian. Yet it also remains possible that this expression may become more exacting and technical. So, for example, we find in Saint Paul's writings the beginnings of a technical form of expression.

Certain words begin to assume a definite meaning in the context in which he uses them, and his theology begins to develop along definite lines.

This possibility of expression cannot be limited only to Scripture, for if it were, then any transformation of culture would mean the end of the expression. Thus it becomes necessary that the expression continue and expand. At the same time there is further intersubjectivity (relationship to the risen Jesus in revelation, the church and the sacraments). This leads again through the literary and technical forms of expression. In other words, there is a kind of spiralling expression. It comes back constantly to the beginning, but at a higher level.

Since this spiral will always involve intersubjective relationship as well as need for expression, the subject himself must change as the progress continues. It involves a constantly spiralling series of conversions (intellectual, moral, religious, Christian). Thus the transformed individual becomes present to himself as transformed, and indeed as transformed beyond human capacities into the realm of the Transcendent. This is what gives intelligibility, I think, to the statement that was made before: Revelation presents us to ourselves, not as we were nor as we could have been, but as we are in its reception. It interprets us. It gives us meaning. Revelation does not merely tell us what we are, but makes us what we are.

It is here that we can also see what is meant by a continuing revelation. While we may speak of the close of revelation at the end of the apostolic era, this is true in the sense of direct intersubjective contact with Jesus now set down in literary form. It does not mean that all intersubjective contact ceases, nor does it mean that its expression is totally set once and for all. There is constant need of both contact and expression, but this present contact and expression will always have as their norm the event of Jesus' coming into the world and its inspired literary expression. This is kept alive and interpreted for all time in the community of the church.

At the level of technical expression this leads to the necessity

of dogmatic and theological development. At the level of intersubjective and incarnate expression it leads to the necessity of
spiritual development. This can be seen exemplified in what was
already said of Saint Teresa. We can now identify this reality as
a dynamic, interpersonal revelation of God, or as a dynamic, interpersonal response of faith. The fact that man is a contingent
being living in time and space means that this dynamism will be
expressed only partially in any given instant. Therefore, what is
at one level the simplicity of God himself is, at another level, the
complexity of man's response in spiritual growth. It is two ways
of looking at one reality.

While this final chapter may seem somewhat speculative and
abstract at times, it is what is said here that has served as the
guiding principle in the preceding chapters. This abstraction
can only receive concrete being in the spiritual life of the individual. We have been called to share in the life of God, and
if we do so we become the place of God's revelation in the world.
This is our duty and our great privilege.

"No one understands the thoughts of God but the Spirit of
God. But the Spirit we have received is not that of the world,
but the Spirit that comes from God, which we have to make us
realize the blessings God has given us... We share the thoughts
of Christ."[6]

---

1. Many of the ideas in these paragraphs are derived from a lecture by
Father Bernard Lonergan. Cf. "Dimensions of Meaning," in *Collection*:
Papers by Bernard Lonergan, S.J., edited by Frederick E. Crowe, S.J., New
York, 1967, pp. 252-267.
2. Lonergan, *op. cit.*, p. 255.
3. What I have to say of horizon is in great measure derived from a talk
delivered by Father David Tracy at a regional meeting of the CTSA in
November, 1967, and from a set of notes taken in his classes and litho-
graphed at the Catholic University of America, 1967 (*Christian Escha-
tology*).
4. "Where knowing is a structure, knowing knowing must be a reduplication
of the structure. Thus if knowing is just looking, then knowing knowing will

be *looking at looking*. But if knowing is a conjunction of experience, understanding and judging, then knowing knowing has to be a conjunction of (1) experiencing experience, understanding and judging, (2) understanding one's experience of experience, understanding and judging, and (3) judging one's experience of experience, understanding and judging to be correct." B. Lonergan, "Cognitional Structure," in *Collection*, p. 224.

5. Intellectual conversion means to appropriate for oneself the "... structure of one's own experiencing, one's own intelligent inquiry and insights, one's own critical reflection and deciding. The crucial issue is an experimental issue, and the experiment will be performed not publicly but privately. It will consist in one's own rational self-consciousness clearly and distinctly taking possession of itself as rational self-consciousness. Up to that decisive achievement all leads. From it all follows... Thoroughly understand what it is to understand, and not only will you understand the broad lines of what there is to be understood but also you will possess a fixed base, an invariant pattern upon all further development of understanding." B. Lonergan, *Insight*, London, 1958, p. xviii.

6. I Cor 2,11-16.